"Moms who are in the spiritual truths ... ~~uun as~~ fuel for the journey of mothering our boys into God's men."

Ginger Nelson
Mayor of the City of Amarillo

"Candy Gibbs has written an inspiring book full of insights about one of life's most important relationships — the one between mothers and sons. Our collective need today for principled individuals and leaders is as high as ever; so, for those wishing to learn more about raising strong sons, Gibbs' book is an engaging and timely read."

Texas State Representative
Four Price & Karen Price

"Preparing and empowering the next generation is essential, and we don't always do this very well. I see it every day in my position — students who are well prepared for the challenges they will experience in college and students who enter this venture ill-prepared. Moms are a real difference maker in this preparation. Great moms love and support their children while also challenging them to grow, learn, and explore. Candy dives into the specific relationship between mom and son, and the opportunity it provides to prepare the son for service to God, to community, to family, and to us all."

James R. Hallmark, Ph.D.
Vice Chancellor for Academic Affairs,
The Texas A&M University System

"This book highlights the power of a mother, walking in her identity, and the plans and purposes of a son being fulfilled. It's a celebration of the complexity, beauty, and strength of the unique relationship between mothers and sons. We have four children, two of whom are boys. Raising men is a high calling, and parenting an act of worship. This book is a tool that exposes fear and arms us with truth."

Pastors Jason & Leanna Craft
Messiah's House, Amarillo TX

"Candy's heartwarming book, *Release,* uses Scripture to console our fears as mothers, while challenging us to take hold of the enormous task that God has uniquely entrusted to us! Her book moves the reader through a full gamut of emotions — from tears to triumph and everything in between — all while reminding us that our job, as mothers of sons, is ultimately to release these young men into the world as great followers of God and great leaders of men."

Todd Lester, Pastor of Forks of Elkhorn
Baptist Church, Midway KY
Kelly Lester, Founder and Chairman of
the Devoted Women's Conference

"Candy has such a simple yet foundational approach to raising children, and I love that she wove Scriptures throughout the book to remind us of our foundation in Christ. It is so important to read and ask questions when we are rearing our children and not just assume that the way we see things is the only and best way. In fact, there are many ways to raise these very individual little people, and I think the more we expose ourselves to information and small groups, the better equipped we are to handle the twists and turns of motherhood!"

Jan Lane, Author of *Strong Women and
the Men Who Love Them*

"Candy Gibbs captures and expounds on the second human organization, after marriage, revealed in Holy Writ — the relationship between a parent and child. The special nature of the relationship between a mother and son can only be understood by a mother and son. She thoughtfully and passionately demonstrates the impact that relationship has when guided by principles from God's Word. As a university president and as a father who watched close-up the relationships of a godly woman with her sons — our sons — this work is critically important. This bond shapes families, families shape communities, and communities shape nations."

Walter V. Wendler, President,
West Texas A&M University

Release

The Art of Fearless Mothering to
Release Powerful and Purposed Sons

CANDY GIBBS

Copyright © 2019 by Candy Gibbs

All rights reserved. No part of this publication may be reproduced, distributed, or transmitted in any form or by any means, including photocopying, recording, or other electronic or mechanical methods, without the prior written permission of the publisher, with the exception of brief quotations embodied in critical reviews and certain other noncommercial uses permitted by copyright law. For permission requests, write to the publisher at the address below.

All examples involving ministry situations are real. However, the details and surrounding circumstances may have been altered or combined to preserve the privacy and confidentiality of the individuals involved.

Unless otherwise noted, Scripture quotations are from the ESV˚ Bible (The Holy Bible, English Standard Version˚). Copyright © 2001 by Crossway, a publishing ministry of Good News Publishers. Used by permission. All rights reserved.

Scripture quotations marked NIV are taken from the Holy Bible, New International Version˚. Copyright 1973, 1978, 1984, 2011 by Biblica, Inc. Used by permission of Zondervan. All rights reserved worldwide. www.Zondervan.com. The NIV and New International Version are trademarks registered in the United States Patent and Trademark Office by Biblica, Inc.˚

Unless otherwise noted, word definitions are taken from the Google dictionary (www.google.com).

Publisher does not have any control over, or responsibility for, any third-party websites referred to in this book. All Internet addresses referred to in this book were correct at the time of going to press. The author and publisher regret any inconvenience caused if addresses have changed or sites have ceased to exist.

For mothers of sons

For all of the broken bones, broken promises, and broken hearts that you mended with such grace. For all of the late nights spent feeding, worrying, and praying. For all the tension in that bow and the courage it took for you to pull back, steady your hand, take a deep breath, and release an arrow on fire with a passion for the Lord — thank you. I am honored to be counted as one of you.

Love, Candy

Contents

Acknowledgments

"I do not cease to give thanks for you, remembering you in my prayers, that the God of our Lord Jesus Christ, the Father of glory, may give you the Spirit of wisdom and of revelation in the knowledge of him."
EPHESIANS 1:16-17

Hope Choice staff and board of directors, thank you so much for your support and prayers. It is truly my privilege to serve with you. I am amazed at your faith to simply step out when our God moves. You are heroes and I am so honored to journey with you.

Susie Merrick, my precious friend, thank you for taking the time in the midst of gracefully walking out a tremendous calling to share your heart with us. I simply love you and you are a fearless, feminine and fierce mother. I want to be just like you when I grow up!

Ana Hoeksema, you are much more than a friend; you are my soul sister in every way. Thank you for pushing on the front end or we would have never made it. I can't wait to see what our God has for those three powerhouse Hoeks boys! Look out, world! Love you so, Ana.

Mallory Cockrell, you are the real MVP and a true ninja! You are a powerful and perfect partner in this thing — that I knew going in. But what continually brings me to my knees is your heart for the Father. You are such a champion for the Kingdom. I would walk onto any battlefield and face any giant next to you. You are family, and I love you so much more than I can convey. Onward, singing louder every step of the way!

Spencer Cockrell, there is no one like you. I am so blessed by you and thankful for you. You are a servant with a warrior heart for the heart of God, as well as gifted at worship, hanging blinds, and choosing the donuts. You are the best!

Kelli Bullard, you are such a professional, diplomatic, precious woman of God and I am better because of our friendship. Thank you for crossing "t's" and dotting "i's" and making me seem much smarter than I am.

Rick and Brenda Trafton, thank you for sharing your retreat with me and for loving me and my family. You are truly family to us and by choice, which is so precious to me. I love you so, and your lives are a beautiful reflection of the Savior. I humbly thank you.

All of you other prayer warriors – and fearless mamas who answered my many questions (you know who you are) – you cannot know what strength and peace came to us through your pouring out your hearts to the Father on our behalf. Where would we be without your sacrifice of prayer before the Lord? Thank you.

Tanner and Jake, I am so proud of the men you are. You are better than your mama could have dreamed you would be. Tan, you are a wonderful daddy to my four grands, and I love watching you love and encourage them. Jake, your passion for students to know the Lord and to live a life worthy of their calling motivates me to be better and work harder for His glory. I love you both so very much, and I am proud to be your mother, boys. Mine you will always be. I am right behind, praying every step of the way. Be great.

ACKNOWLEDGMENTS

Brian Gibbs, I know I said I would never write another book, and well... You are the visionary and courage of this outfit. Thank you for dealing with my excitement and my meltdowns. Without you, I would not be me. I love you.

Madison, my girl, what will I do with you so far away? You are a beautiful balance of strength and grace, and you are my dear and precious friend. I am honored to be your mom. I love you, Madio.

Lord Jesus, oh the steps we have taken together. You have always allowed me to feel the weight of the bow and the tension in the string, just enough to trust You to pull back a tad bit more. These arrows in their mama's bow have flown strong and true, all because of You. I love You with all that I am and all that I hope to become. Thank You for helping me to release and for standing with me through it all.

So honored to have experienced this journey with each of you!!

Foreword

BY SUSIE MERRICK
WORSHIP LEADER, MENTOR, MOTHER AND GRANDMOTHER

I always wanted to be a mom. I never thought I wouldn't be one, and I never felt it wasn't enough. I was part of a family in which my own mother gave birth to five children all by the time she was 29 years old! So you can see why it never entered my mind that I couldn't do it. I just didn't think much about how important it is to do it right.

Growing up, I had a close family, and my mother and father modeled respect for each other. Because I was raised in a happy home, I naturally mothered much the same way my mother did. Her advice was solid, and it was based on plenty of experience. But what I came to realize was that just as my parents raised me and my siblings the way God led them, my husband and I needed to find God's will and plan for our family as well.

I'm not an author, and I don't qualify as an expert on family or boys. I'm simply a mother who has gone to the Lord every day that I can remember concerning all four of our children. My husband, Garth, and I have two sons and two daughters. They are all grown now, and although the relationship with them has changed, one thing never will. We will always be their mother and father, and they will always be our children. We have a place in their lives and they have a place in ours. However, we still need encouragement from the truth of God's Word.

As I've looked at my relationship with my sons, I realize there is a dynamic like no other relationship. As Christian mothers, we have a great responsibility to demonstrate how godly strength and tenderness looks in a family, at school, in a job, and in relationship with others.

In doing so, I've had to face my insecurities, admit that I was wrong, and ask for forgiveness over and over again.

Mothers need help, and we need it from the One who made our sons to be our sons! We need God to show us and teach us how to release them to Him, the One who loves them even more than we can.

Candy Gibbs is a woman of God. She cares about what God cares about. She has written from what she has experienced firsthand in raising her own sons, and I admire her for being determined to pull back the curtain and reveal the Truth that we all need so desperately. In this book, *Release,* she has taken a giant step to bring encouragement and revelation to this unique bond between mothers and sons.

She has shined the light of Truth on the deception of the enemy. Too often we ARE afraid and insecure when it comes to our relationship with our sons, and yet it was God's divine design for mothers to be the first female in their lives. We are appointed to be successful at raising sons!

Candy has also addressed the spirit of fear: it is a liar! But she doesn't stop there. She lets us hear the truth about who we really are, which brings peace and confidence to a mother's heart. She reminds us that we are not disqualified!

Even if you weren't raised in a healthy environment, even if you didn't know the Lord when your children were born, and even if you're beginning your journey as you read this book, you are invited to experience the right path to a healthy relationship with your sons!

PART I
Introduction

Preface

"Mothers and their children are in a category all their own.
There's no bond so strong in the entire world. No love so
instantaneous and forgiving."

GAIL TSUKIYAMA, *DREAMING WATER*

Well — here we are again. I don't know if I want to burst into tears or laugh myself right off of this porch. Just three years ago (seems more like three minutes ago), I sat viewing beautiful mountains as I put the final period on our book, *Rescue*. I have never shouted louder, longer, or with more authentic joy than I did when that project was finished.

First let me say, writing does not come easily to me. I am not articulate, and I am the worst English student ever to walk the planet. I don't really have *time* to write. I am the Executive Director of a ministry, and I am privileged that the Lord allows me to travel and speak some of the time. I have a busy family, and I love my church and my community.

Writing keeps me up at night. I worry. I schedule time to work on the project and how many of you know that when I decide that I will write next Wednesday afternoon for four hours, that next Wednesday afternoon I have absolutely nothing to say! I mean, not one meaningful thought comes into my scrawny head.

The subject matter of *Rescue* was overwhelming. We discussed pornography, sexuality, relationships, struggle, middle school, college, and faith — and we did it with a group of young adults we called the Lifeguards, that I grew to love deeply. They were opinionated and passionate and, man, were they wise. That book is still ministering to families in very dark and difficult waters, but the process of it took all I had. We worked together with the Lifeguards over an 18-month period. Finally, one weekend in June of 2014, I loaded up the car with my son Jake and daughter Madi, and we headed to the mountains for five days that were dedicated to finishing my part of the book. Only my family knew that along with all my material and my computer, I had a letter to my board of directors apologizing to them and explaining that it was too much and I just simply could not finish the project. I told my family I would either finish the book during that time or I would mail the letter. By the grace of God and with the help and encouragement of my family, our Hope Choice team and the Lifeguards, I didn't mail the letter — and the work those young adults put in has been a lifeline to many drowning families.

As I drove home from that mountaintop experience, I made it very clear to the Lord that I was setting aside my laptop and had no intention of ever going through the editing process again. I meant it too. With every new gray hair, I meant it. The Lord let me live there for a season and since that time, my son Tanner and his family have joined the Air Force and are stationed far away. Jake has graduated from high school and is attending Texas A&M and my Madi-girl is starting college. Hope Choice continues to increase in scope of ministry, and the Lord has been so faithful to provide for us to do the work He has given us. Generally, things were going well, and then, you know exactly what I am going to say: there came the nudging.

"Please, Lord, ask someone else," I pleaded. There are so many people who have more experience than I do, and they probably enjoy writing! Please don't ask me to write something else. I would rather climb Mt. Everest, run a marathon, or just enjoy another cup of coffee in the mornings with the small amount of extra time I have on my hands. OK, so I wouldn't climb Mt. Everest or run a marathon, but an extra cup of coffee sounds heavenly! Why do I have to write?

I finally began to spend some time praying about what the Lord might be asking me to do and when I felt that He had laid the subject matter on my heart I decided that the second book needed to be written.

I love that the Father's plan for us is centered around family. He tells us that it is not good for man to be alone. We need people to journey with us. Our good God loves family Himself. He is our Father. Our Lord and Savior is the very Son of God. He calls us His own and grafts us into His family though the spirit of sonship.

For as long as I can remember, I wanted to be a mom. I love kids and really always have. I imagined what it would all look like: how I would arrange our home, the routine of the day for my babies, play dates and snowcones, jammies and puppies, Bible stories and bathtime. I always wanted to be the best mom ever — to be supermom.

What is a supermom anyway?

Since the day I married my husband and took the hand of my new son Tanner who was five at the time, the desire of my heart has been to be a good mom. I look around at many of the mothers who are nothing short of extraordinary and — yikes!

My sister is a supermom. She makes the most amazing snacks for all three of her daughters' classes for every party or holiday. She bakes and she crafts. She was a collegiate volleyball player and even coached on the high school and college level. Now, as a stay-at-home mom, she is the most amazing club volleyball coach you can imagine. She is the room mom and the birthday party planner extraordinaire. She is amazing and is truly a supermom.

My mentor, Brenda, is a supermom. She *is Better Homes and Gardens.* She has a beautiful home. She has an immaculate yard. She is gentle, kind, positive, loving, and focused in like a laser beam on her love relationship with Christ. She has walked the walk of a godly marriage and family. She is the mother of two wonderful and gifted children and has four grandchildren. She is lovely. She has the most elegant fashion sense and always looks adorable. She is all things "mother," and I love her dearly. She is a supermom.

My friend, Lynne, is a supermom. She has three children with busy lives. She is always up for the next adventure. She engages her children; she is a supportive and loving wife. She enjoys time with her friends and balances all of those things in an amazing way. She has a mother-daughter tea at Christmastime, plays racquetball, and serves as the leader of a large Bible study group. She is a supermom.

I have always wanted to be a supermom, but…

I am not particularly crafty. I have been known to glue my hands together with super glue on more than one occasion, and have literally taken pictures of my friends' pumpkin arrangements so I could decorate my own porch for fall.

PREFACE

I am not always positive. I try hard, but I can certainly get overwhelmed. My children have seen tears roll down my face on many occasions as we race from one thing to the next, hoping that I remembered to turn the oven off before we ran out the door. I am too busy. I have gone to pick the kids up from school and, distracted by a phone call, driven off before they actually got in the car. Who does that??

I am not a gardener. I want to be. I can't tell you how much time and money I have spent on flowers, seeds, and bulbs for my flower beds. I can study it too, using a measuring tape to place the seeds and bulbs the precise distance from each other in just the right amount of sun. You'd be surprised to know that if you drove by my house.

I struggle with fashion. I am not great at fixing hair. I don't like animals. I am an OK cook, but I'm no Martha Stewart. I like to play all kinds of sports with my kids, but they are all better than I am, so I can't offer much advice. I am not musical and not very sophisticated.

I think being a supermom may never be checked off my bucket list. So I have decided to just be mom to Tanner, Jake, and Madi. I am going to focus on the abilities that the Lord gave *me* as a mom. I love my kids. I enjoy just sitting and talking with them. I love to journal back and forth. When they are home, we still read the Bible together in the mornings and enjoy watching movies together with popcorn and blankets. I imagine what the Lord has called them to be and strive to help them see those things in themselves. I am their biggest fan. No matter what they are participating in, I want them to look in the crowd and see me. I am conscientious about making memories and desire that my family would

7

look back on the years that our heads hit the pillow under the same roof and remember that we laughed a lot, we accomplished some good, and we loved each other.

I am not a perfect mom, not a supermom, and likely neither are you. Let's give ourselves permission to just be the moms that He has equipped us to be. Sounds pretty super to me.

I have noticed something over the past 20 years of family and mothering: we can almost place our fingers on the relationships in our family and literally trace the fingerprint of the Father. He expresses Himself in relationship. He defines Himself through family. He connects. He interacts. He instructs. He plays. He binds up our broken hearts. He defends and protects. He challenges and asks us to trust Him. He rests and He watches. He speaks and He listens. He teaches us to need others. He promises us a beautiful inheritance. We can even see the twinkle in His eye as He declares His own inheritance to be us. He loves.

Family is a beautiful thing. After all, the Father's heart is to be reconciled with us, and that is the very reason He sent His Son to be our sacrifice. That's how much our Father values family. I can't help but imagine what must have gone through the Father's thoughts as He prepared for the day He placed His Beloved into His purpose. He must have thought something like, "My Son will need a journey mate. Someone who will be gentle enough to teach him how to obey, to be a good friend and to serve. Someone insightful enough to understand that, after all, Jesus is the Word and was there from the beginning. Someone humble enough to teach His Son how to plant and tend a garden, knowing full well Jesus could speak it straight into harvest time. Someone wise enough to allow Him to question and to grow in wisdom and stature with Me and men. His journey mate will need to be strong enough to endure grief that literally rips the heart to pieces in a way that no other human being can comprehend and allow Him to fulfill His purpose. This journey mate will be the first face He sees as He enters the world and the last He will see as she walks Him back home. The person My Son needs for this journey is a mom."

Over the course of the next few pages we will share together, I want to focus on the unique relationship between mothers and sons. Raising these mighty men is not for the faint of heart, and you can say that again! But what a high calling! I will share with you some insights from some extraordinary mothers in my life and share some of our stories along the way as well.

One of my most favorite Scriptures in all of God's Word is Luke 2:19: *"But Mary treasured up all these things and pondered them in her heart"* (NIV).

I have treasured in my heart more than 20 years of memories with my boys, and I don't want to take any of them for granted. I trust that as we begin this journey, we will laugh together over ripped jeans and spilled milk and will shed some tears over breakups, broken noses, and the drive home from college drop-off. I am honored to have you as a journey mate because, as the mom of a son or two, I appreciate the blood on your blouse, the tear in your eye, and the love in your heart for that ball of Kingdom power that you call "son."

Shall we begin?

Fearless Motherhood

"Perhaps it takes courage to raise children."
JOHN STEINBECK, *EAST OF EDEN*

"Guard the good deposit that was entrusted to you – guard it with the help of the Holy Spirit who lives in us."
2 TIMOTHY 1:14 (NIV)

I am a girl (obviously) and my only sibling is a very precious younger sister. There were no boys in our home except for our dad, and he isn't *really* a "boy." Growing up, our home was full of laughter, many tears, fights over clothes, late night talks involving way too much chocolate, lessons on hair and make-up, sports, lots of boyfriends, great girlfriend memories, and talking — lots and lots of talking.

When Brian and I married, I immediately became mom to a five-year-old boy. Not long after that, along came Jake, and then there were two. Two boys. What in the world was the Lord thinking? I have no experience with this. I may not have the stomach for it, either. How am I going to be the mom to these two boys? Fear set in.

It is my opinion that fear is one of the only, and certainly one of the strongest, tools of the enemy. Think back over your life as a mom. How many times has the card the enemy played been one of fear? Fear mostly of the future. How will this turn out and what horrible role will I have played in my son's demise simply because I don't know what I am doing as a mom?

I look back over our life as a family and I can recall numerous occasions when in the midst of a difficult situation I would think, "Now would be the perfect time for a pause button. I need a moment because I am looking into the dirty face of a boy who is still panting from that very dangerous, crazy yet perfect backflip off of the trampoline. I need to pause this moment until I know the right 'mom' thing to say!"

Or have you ever had the thought, "We really need an adult right now and I think I may be the best we've got"? The enemy is so crafty at making us feel inadequate and thus paralyzing us with fear. He has a plan. If He can make us afraid, he can render us *powerless*. When we are afraid, we freeze not knowing what the right next move is. Our fear becomes our focus and causes us to shrink back and be distracted from our calling or the callings placed on our children.

> "For the spirit God gave us does not make us timid [or fearful], but gives us power, love and self-discipline."
>
> 2 Timothy 1:7 (NIV)

Fear is a spirit and a prophetic spirit, at that. It tells you about your future or the future of your family and your children. First of all, our enemy does not know our future. He knows his because he can read about it! Because Satan knows how this ends, he is relentless in his pursuit, which is to steal, kill, and destroy. When we base our decisions about our children on the lies the spirit of fear tells us, we will be rendered impotent and powerless.

So where does the enemy snare us? What are we afraid of as moms?

First, we are afraid of our children. I know that sounds super silly, that we are afraid of our own children, but take a moment to think about it. How many times have we made parental decisions based on how our children will respond? Are they going to rebel? What if they hate us? They are going to quite literally throw a fit.

Remember when these young men were cute little boys? We have all had the experience of our sons asking for ice cream or a candy bar. As moms, we know that saying no is going to result in an ugly and embarrassing fit. When our sons were two, though it was definitely uncomfortable, we were willing to face the fit for the good of our sons. Why then does that change when they are 15? Let me assure you that it is as natural for a 15-year-old to throw a fit as it is for a two-year-old. However, these fits are quite a bit more overwhelming to us moms. Sometimes we base our decisions on our fear of the fit.

This spirit of fear has convinced us that *all* teenagers rebel. If we are too strict, we will push them into doing the very thing we don't want them to do, and our children, especially when they are teens, will not want anything to do with us.

Not one of those statements is true. Not all teenagers rebel. All kids make mistakes but the vast majority of them do not go hog wild. I am not talking about being overly strict or legalistic, but can I tell you that if you are allowing things in your home that make you uncomfortable because you are afraid of how your children will respond if you set a standard — that is called blackmail.

We do not parent our children based on how they will or will not respond. Parenting is an act of worship and is directly tied to my relationship with the Lord. When a situation happens, I go to the Lord and I do what He tells me to do. The way my child responds is up to him and his relationship with God. For example, say that my son wants to date a young woman. Brian and I go to the Lord about it, and we will base our decision on the direction of the Holy Spirit. It has nothing to do with being strict, but fear of our children's response must not blackmail us into making decisions that are detrimental to our children and disobedient to the Lord.

The second thing we fear is what other people, especially other moms, will think. The spirit of fear has us convinced that our friends will think we are "those" parents, and that our children will not have any friends if we don't give them a cell phone in the third grade and let them have an Instagram account. We cannot continue to look to the right or to the left to see how others are parenting and base our decisions on them. We cannot mother out of a fear of what our friends will say about us.

"Do not love the world or the things in the world. If anyone loves the world, the love of the Father is not in him. For all that is in the world — the desires of the flesh and the desires of the eyes and the pride of life — is not from the Father but is from the world.

And the world is passing away along with its desires, but whoever does the will of God abides forever."

1 John 2:15-17

The truth is — who cares what your friends think of the decisions you are making in your home? We experience peer pressure as much as our children do. Do not be afraid to think for yourself. Let your yes be yes and your no be no, and know why you take the stands you do. If it is because that is how the Lord is directing your family, then stick to it. Your children will be better off if your decisions about technology, social media, dating, etc. are based on your relationship with the Lord and His Word rather than the opinion of Mrs. Jones across the street.

Finally, we are afraid that we are messing this up — that we don't know how to do this "mom" thing. The spirit of fear whispers things such as, "Oh wow, what if your children were to find out about those things you've done in your past? How in the world can you set a higher standard for your children than you were able to keep at their age? You aren't even smart enough to help with 7th grade homework, and you are the best these kids have for learning about life? You don't trust yourself. Why should they trust you? This is like the blind leading the blind here. You can't see the direction you and your family should be heading any better than your three-year-old can."

"This is the message we have heard from Him and declare to you: God is light; in Him there is no darkness at all. If we claim to have fellowship with Him and yet walk in the darkness, we lie and do not live

15

out the truth. But if we walk in the light, as He is in the light, we have fellowship with one another, and the blood of Jesus, His Son, purifies us from all sin."

1 John 1:5-7 (NIV)

God is light and in Him there is no darkness at all. We need to begin to speak to our fear: "You listen here, you spirit of fear. This is not the blind leading the blind. This is the once blind but now fully-sighted child of the Most High God, one forgiven by the blood of Christ that purified me from all of my sin, walking in the light with Him. And I see you for who you are. God has not given me a spirit of fear, but of power, love and a sound mind!"

From where I am sitting we are in the battle of our lifetime for our sons — really all of our children. We are in a battle for our very way of life. And fear has rendered us powerless and impotent.

As believers who are part of the body of Christ, here is what is true about you:

- **You are the guardian of your son's dreams.** So until his heart is strong enough to chase his dreams, you must be strong enough for the both of you.

- **You are a carrier of hope.** *"But hope that is seen is no hope at all. Who hopes for what they already have? But if we hope for what we do not yet have, we wait for it patiently"* (Romans 8:24–25 NIV). You see hope when he sees discouragement. Speak hope over him.

- **You are a mentor and an example.** Your son watches you. He takes notice when difficulties arise and you

16

keep your eyes on Christ. He notices when you keep your word to a friend when it would have been easier to forget it. He sees you working hard to steer your family in the right direction. He will follow you as you follow Christ.

- **You are a piece of his strength.** Both of our sons wrestled. In a difficult wrestling match, it is hard for me to watch as they struggle and fight. But one thing is sure: no matter how hard it is for me, there will not be a match where my son can't find me. In adversity, your son needs to find you in his crowd. Just your locking eyes with him will communicate to his heart, "You look right here, son; I am proud of you. You are strong; you can do it."

- **You give life.** Life and death are in the power of your tongue. When your son falls and gets bruises and skinned knees, you are the voice saying, "Let me help you up; let me dust you off. Now, you try again."

- **You are a mirror.** You see things in your son that are too extraordinary for him to comprehend. You act as a mirror that reflects back to him the greatness that you see in him, and you keep holding that mirror in front of him until he can see that greatness for himself.

- **You are his protector.** You will stand guard and you will stand against every attack of the enemy that comes against him. You will continue to fight intense battles through prayer without growing weary in doing good. You are a mom.

These descriptions do not sound like powerless, fearful people. These descriptions sound like a strong, competent, secure, powerful, bold, beautiful warrior for the Kingdom, and that, my dear sister, is you!!!

I would like to close this chapter with a prayer for you.

"God, thank You that we are armed for battle. You have given us the sword of the spirit; Your Word and Your favor protect us like a shield. We are not afraid. We are not afraid! We will stand where You have called us to stand, and we will be fierce in the protection of our children. We will be fierce in our love for You first, for our spouses and for our children. God, we will not be silent, and we are not weak because Your Holy Spirit is alive in us. Your Word is active in us.

"God, help us to stay submitted to the authorities You have placed over us, but Lord, in the name of Jesus we will stand at our post. We will fight the battles that come our way and we will take ground for Your Kingdom. The enemy will not have our families; he will not have our marriages, and he will not have our sons. The battle is Yours, and we need only to stand. We will stop denying there *is* a battle and we will wield our swords. Make us strong, alert, and dangerous to the enemy.

"You are the Victor. We are honored to come alongside You and humbled that You would allow us this privilege.. Make us different. In the mighty name of Jesus, Amen."

You are handpicked to mother this young man. You are just the mom to do it. Let's do it without fear. You are fully equipped for this good work the Lord has prepared in advance for you.

18

PART II
Heritage

2

Samuel

Heritage – "an allotted portion"

I decided to start this section of the book with a biblical story I have always loved deeply. I love the sentiment of the story of Hannah and Samuel, a mama and her boy. I am in awe of this mother's strength that she passed on to her son, and the disciple that he became, I believe in part because of the heritage of faithful obedience he received from his mother. Most mornings when I pray for my sons and for Madi, I pray for your children as well. I ask the Lord to raise up a generation of Samuels — a generation that will learn to hear the voice of the Lord at a young age and then obey His Word all the days of their lives.

But we can't examine Samuel's "allotted portion" without taking a look at his mother.

"After they had eaten and drunk in Shiloh, Hannah rose. Now Eli the priest was sitting on the seat beside the doorpost of the temple of the Lord. She was deeply distressed and prayed to the Lord and wept bitterly. And she vowed a vow and said, 'O Lord of hosts, if

you will indeed look on the afflictions of your servant and remember me and not forget your servant, but will give to your servant a son, then I will give him to the Lord all the days of his life, and no razor shall touch his head.' As she continued praying before the Lord, Eli observed her mouth. Hannah was speaking in her heart; only her lips moved, and her voice was not heard. Therefore Eli took her to be a drunken woman. And Eli said to her, 'How long will you go on being drunk? Put your wine away from you.' But Hannah answered, 'No, my lord, I am a woman troubled in spirit. I have drunk neither wine nor strong drink, but I have been pouring out my soul before the Lord.'"

1 Samuel 1:9-15

Hannah was in a difficult season of her life, unable to this point to have a child. As I read these words, they are very personal to me. I had three pregnancies that all ended in loss before Jake was born. I wanted to carry a baby desperately and often my conversations with the Lord were consumed with that longing. Every mother has experienced some season in life that was difficult and has felt desperate. My prayer is that we would learn from Hannah. In the overwhelming, hopeless and desperate moments of our lives, may we press in close to the Lord and not move further away. That's what Hannah did; in complete and vulnerable authenticity, she poured out her soul to the Lord. Something else that strikes me about Hannah's story is that from the moment she asked the Lord for a son, she began releasing her son back to the Father.

"I prayed for this child, and the Lord has granted me what I asked of him. So now I give him to the Lord. For his whole life, he will be given over to the Lord."

1 Samuel 1: 27-28 (NIV)

I am going to give you just my idea of what may have happened in Samuel's early years. From what we know about Hannah as a mother, I think it may have gone something like this. Samuel was likely under the age of five when he went to live and serve at the temple. But up until that time, I can imagine Hannah snuggling up by a fire with sweet little Samuel as she recounted to him her desperate cries to the Lord that He would bless her with a son. I bet they giggled over the fact that Eli thought something was wrong with Hannah that she was crying so much.

I am sure that Hannah would have expressed to Samuel over and over that he was her heritage, her allotted portion — that the Lord answered her cry for a son by the gift of Samuel himself. I am sure she must have shared with Samuel what an incredible purpose the Lord must have for him, being that he was the answer to such an earnest prayer. Hannah began to make memories with Samuel very young, because her moments with him would be few. Samuel was listening.

Hannah would have shared with Samuel that even in the moments in our lives when we don't understand what the Lord is doing or we feel like He is distant, those are the moments that we move in close and do not pull back. She would have told him, "The Lord Himself is our inheritance. He rises to show us compassion, so when you are afraid or alone, Samuel, move in closer to Him." Samuel was listening.

Finally the day came when Hannah would make good on her word to the Lord. She took Samuel to the temple to be given to the Lord and to serve Him all of his life. I am sure she must have explained it to Samuel to the best of her ability. You know that she would have told him again and again that it was out of her great love for the Lord and for Samuel that he would need to live at the temple with Eli. I know her mind understood it, but I struggle to even grasp the strength that it must have taken for this diligent, faithful mother who had been relentless in her pursuit of a son, to take the same little Samuel, her allotted portion, and deliver him to his new home. Samuel watched his mother demonstrate obedience and immense strength.

Hannah was discipling her son. She was demonstrating for him what it means to draw near to God, to listen for His Word in our lives and to obey Him, to make memories and mark them in our hearts and minds, to ask the Lord to grant us the strength to fulfill our purpose. Hannah understood what it meant to model a life submitted to the Lord and obedience even when it defies our own desires. Hannah was discipling her son who would become a great prophet of the Most High. Not only would Samuel eventually anoint Saul the first King of Israel, but he would also be the one chosen to anoint King David.

Samuel received a beautiful inheritance from his mother. We see Samuel as a young child, sleeping in the presence of the Lord and hearing Him speak, not just any word but a difficult one, and then sharing that with Eli. We see Samuel demonstrating strength in obedience when he anointed David as king. Samuel loved Saul, and it was hurtful to him to hear the Lord say that Saul would no longer be king. In fact, Samuel was instructed to go anoint the next king who happened to be a son of Jesse. Samuel didn't want to hurt his friend, Saul, but still he obeyed the Lord. Samuel was a disciple, a follower of the Lord all of his days, and he is a giant in the faith.

Not only did Samuel receive a spiritual inheritance from his mother, but he also received her blessing. There is something powerful about a blessing. Jacob stole one and then later wrestled with God for a real one. Abraham prayed that not only Isaac but Ishmael, too, would live under the blessing of the Almighty. The priests pronounced them, and the Israelite people (as well as you and I) walk under a blessing. A blessing can solidify our course and can provide encouragement and hope when things don't seem to be going as planned.

I recently saw a text that started me thinking. I have a beautiful family. Oh, believe me, we are not perfect and have our fair share of mistakes and difficulty in our midst. But something that is precious to me — more precious than words can do justice — is the spiritual blessing and inheritance that my maternal grandparents have spoken over us and walked out in good times and in bad. I never had a meal with my Papa (my maternal grandfather) that we didn't pray. I remember him serving as a deacon in his church for as far back as my memories go. He taught a Sunday school class, and there wasn't a day of the week that you would catch him when he wasn't studying for that coming week's lesson. For forty years, not one Christmas Eve passed without his family listening as he read the story of Christ's birth. My Papa was the spiritual patriarch of our family. He passed away a few years ago, and the memories and the blessing of his life mean more to me than these pages can contain.

Not long before he passed away, I saw a text from my Papa to my son. The text said, "You have my blessing." So much beauty, honor and power is contained in that short sentence that it sent me straight to my knees. My Papa, blessing my teenage son and saying to him, "Our family's feet are firmly planted on this path. Go and take the land the Lord has given you, and make an impact for His great Kingdom. You have my blessing."

I wonder if we should be more deliberate in giving our blessing? I am not talking about giving our OK or permission. I mean, have we spoken over our children and declared their spiritual inheritance? Your family has been given an inheritance, and it is certainly beautiful. The Father loves family and legacy. Remind your sons today whose they are and of the land He's called them to. They can change the world; sometimes they just need to be reminded that it is in their bloodline. They are heirs of the King, and they have your blessing.

One of my favorite verses in the Bible is a quote from Mary. Jesus and Mary were attending a wedding, and this turned out to be Jesus' first miracle. The wedding party had run out of wine. Mary went to Jesus and told him of the dilemma.

"And Jesus said to her, 'Woman, what does this have to do with me? My hour has not yet come.'

His mother said to the servants, 'Do whatever he tells you.'"

John 2:4–5

What a precious exchange between mother and son we see in this moment with Jesus and Mary. Mary goes to her son with a request, knowing full well that it gives Jesus great pleasure to meet her needs. When he says, "Mom, why are you bringing me into this?" Mary doesn't say another thing to Jesus. She turns to the servants, and I think with a sparkle in her eye, says, "Just do whatever He tells you."

That is Hannah's message to Samuel: Son, no matter what and come what may, you press in to His Presence, and just do whatever He tells you. Over the next few pages, we will follow Hannah's and Samuel's example. We will make memories. We will learn to watch our Savior, listen for His Voice, and become disciples even when that warrants a great amount of strength.

Our sons are our heritage, our allotted portion, and we are passing on to them a spirit-filled blessing and powerful inheritance. May they always press in, listen, demonstrate strength and "just do whatever He tells them."

3

Making Memories

"Enjoy the little things because one day you may look back and realize they were the big things."
ROBERT BRAULT

I am not good at many things. I didn't seem to show up on the right day that the Lord handed out talent. But one thing I got was a double dose of the intense desire to know each one of my children to the very deepest part of their being and to love them fiercely. I can tell what kind of day Madi has had from a five-second glance across a crowded gym. I know how Tanner is doing by the height of his grin. When Jake calls, I know where his heart is by the way he inhales before saying hello. But that's what moms do, right?

I realized recently how much time has escaped me. With Tanner now married and a father himself and Jake and Madi both college students, I am overwhelmed with disbelief that we have actually lived every minute of their lives and it now seems like it was only a few short breaths.

As moms, we want events, gatherings and memories to be perfect, from the cinnamon rolls to the decorations! But I have learned that what I remember is not how perfect the dinner or the house was, but rather the moments with those

I love most. Beyond the struggle for perfection lies an inward posture of rest and peace that finds contentment in the "done," that what has been done is enough. Whatever season you are in, developing a relationship with your son is about time together and memories — it's about being in this moment. Mary understood this better than anyone in Scripture. She learned the art of being present in and remembering the moment.

I can't help wondering how Mary must have felt. From the moment the angel announced she would have a son, she knew that time would escape her. The precious baby she cared for, taught how to walk and talk, and tucked in at night... the son she threw the ball to, taught how to clear the table, and watched as he walked off to school. The young man she saw turn water to wine, silence the learned and religious, and raise the dead...her son, her God, her Savior was with her on borrowed time. I wonder how she felt when she heard He had been arrested. What was she thinking as she watched the man He had become — the son that she loved, raised and worshipped — be questioned and tortured?

We know she was there. As difficult as it must have been for her to watch, could she have been anywhere else? She was there the moment He drew His first breath and she would be there when He drew His last. Many of those who had followed Him, who loved Him, were there. But she was His mama; there was nowhere else on the planet she would be but there, at His feet. When He was weak and hurting, He could find her. He could see the love in her eyes.

I for one will take a lesson from Mary. I will resist the urge to make gatherings "perfect" and in so doing, miss the gathering myself all together. I will not allow my thoughts to revert to the relationships that are painful, the people that I miss, or the presents I didn't buy. I will remember that "there is no tomorrow." There is only this moment.

I will watch the glow in my family's eyes as they experience the wonder of His majesty. I will watch for those special moments to etch in my memory as they talk, laugh and cry together. I will remember that we are on borrowed time. And they will be able to find me, in this moment, and see the love in my eyes. Where else on the planet would I be?

I would have to agree with some of you that "now" is my favorite stage with my children. I have loved every season, and the relationships with our children can become deeper and sweeter with every passing year. As a mom looking ahead to raising teenagers, it can appear to be daunting and overwhelming. But take it from those of us who are standing on the other side of that season when we tell you that those years can be fulfilling and full of reward. I look forward to daily conversations about how the day was and just the simple things that made them laugh or were difficult. We laugh together and often I have a few tears. I want to know my children's hearts. That is what makes each stage the best. To look into their lives and see where they have been and what He is accomplishing in them now is like breathing in a deep breath of fresh air. "Now" is the only place to be.

Realizing the importance of being in this moment hit me suddenly one winter night when Jake was in the 6th grade. We were watching a Christmas movie and the thought crossed my mind: *I have only 6 more Christmases with him living at home.* All of the things that I wanted to do and conversations I wanted to have before he left home washed over me in waves. Once I pulled it together, I became very intentional about creating memories and traditions. I desired that the sights, sounds, smells and tastes would always remind my children of home and that they are deeply loved. Our children, sons included, gain security and courage to live fully when they have the support and connection to their family, mamas in particular.

In a blink, my youth escaped me, and I am in the full throes of being a wife and a mom and even a GiGi. I am amazed at how quickly my life has evolved from being about what I wanted to be when I grew up to trying to figure out how to be all grown up with grace, truth and energy. My head spins to think about my babies learning to walk and talk and then to realize that they are now in college and having children of their own!

I was thinking about that very thing recently while running from one place to the next, trying to keep up with all of the craziness of this busy family. I was remembering the days of naps, car seats, and bedtime stories and suddenly a thought just fell into my mind: "I would play more." The one thing I would do differently about my children's toddler and preschool years is this. I would play.

Life is too short, and we take ourselves so seriously. I would have learned earlier how to cherish moments and be fully in them. I decided to just make a short list for all of you young moms, take them or leave them.

Let your children play in the rain and jump in the puddles.

Laugh at puppies.

Take a nap with them.

Take a lot of pictures.

Listen to them; don't tune them out.

Let them climb a tree.

Don't fight their battles.

Lie by them at night.

Sing lots of songs.

Leave the dishes and take a walk in the park.

Don't take them to school before they are ready.

On *those* mornings when milk gets spilled, the washing machine overflows and you forget to make the brownies, just be late. The world keeps turning.

When your sons are little and full of life, a popsicle on the back porch and walk around the block slaying dragons will leave sweet traces in their memory. Don't miss the simple opportunities for them to recall what their mom looked like while on the lookout for a T-Rex or what you smelled like on your Sunday morning drive to church. As a mom who has spent more of my moments than some of you, take it from me. I don't regret one time of putting duties aside for memories, but I regret several times I chose not to.

As those little boys become young men, you may need to get a little more creative in your memory making. One of my favorite things about my son Tanner is that he enjoys life. He loves to laugh, and he's quite funny. Everyone feels like they are Tanner's favorite person. When Tanner turned 14, the Lord gave me a brilliant idea for bonding with him which has become one of my favorite traditions. I got up at 2:00 a.m.

and put blankets in the dryer. Much to his chagrin, I woke him and had him come outside with me. I wrapped him up in a warm blanket and we laid on the front lawn together. We bonded that night and many late nights to follow. Now, Tanner lives hundreds of miles away from me, but we share sweet memories of times spent together while the world slept. No amount of years or miles can take that away from us.

Jake is a deep thinker and very deliberate. He is on time and on point, always. One thing I respect greatly about Jake is that even if his next appointment is pressing, if he is in a conversation with you or you are needing his attention, you have it 100% and he won't cut the time short. The reason I respect that so much is that it goes against his type A, driven personality. I know that when he chooses to ignore the clock and focus on our conversation, he is being deliberate, he's being present in the moment, and he values our relationship. My sons have learned that moments are priceless and valuable because we have lost some very special people in our lives — my mother (Grandmom) and my grandfather (Papa). Jake counts the time he had with them as precious, and he does a great job of creating memories with people he loves.

One more thing to consider as your boys get older: it is good to set expectations about what you both hope for your relationship to be. Here are some of the things that I have shared with my sons that are important to me: I like to talk to Jake on the phone every day, even if it's brief. Just hearing his voice helps me to know how he is doing. Tanner knows that I value a "spend the night" with his family around Christmas. It may not always be on Christmas Eve, which I understand, but an overnight with Pop and GiGi is high on my list.

Our sons likely aren't as verbal as we are, and they may not even realize how much they treasure certain memories and traditions. Don't think that they can read your mind; they can't. If we are perfectly honest, sometimes we don't even understand what we are feeling. So, tell him. Explain to him what your hopes and expectations are for your relationship. He will do his best to accommodate and even if he doesn't articulate it, chances are that time with you is important to him as well.

Remember, moms, as you set out to make memories for your sons. It rarely will come out "perfect" but it will be beautiful nonetheless. Also, it isn't always the big ones — Christmas, birthdays or vacations — that leave the sweetest mark on our hearts. Sometimes it is sitting on the lawn at 2:00 a.m., Saturday morning donuts, or a glance and shared grin with a sweaty boy on a wrestling mat that you'll never forget. Make memories. Cherish them, and teach that young man of yours to do the same.

Strength

"Satan never wastes a fiery dart on an area covered in armor."
BETH MOORE

Wow. Been feeling the sting of a fiery dart lately? I must admit that sometimes one hits me when I least expect it. I'm not sure how theologically correct this is, but in my mind fiery darts from the enemy are those thoughts that unexpectedly invade a perfectly fine day.

Maybe it's an accusation about something from the past or, even more painful, the thought that someone may find out about something from the past. It could be a fear of a choice a son may make or the fear of the embarrassment that choice may cause. It could be the smallest doubt of the reality of salvation, or that lingering fear that a husband may be spending a little too much time with his secretary or his nurse. Could be insecurity about the future or anxiety about balancing the checking account. It could be one of a multitude of small thoughts that with a quick release from the enemy hits us in an area of vulnerability and throws us completely off course.

As Brian and I have raised these two sons of ours who are both now off living their own adventures, I promise you we could open our own used sporting goods store. With all the "gear" stored in our garage, attic, out buildings and closets, we wouldn't have to restock inventory for a couple of years! We have helmets for football, baseball, and bike riding. We have bows and arrows, BB guns, airsoft guns and targets. We have basketballs, baseballs and footballs. We have wrestling mats, knee pads and shoes of any size you can imagine. We have catcher's gear and gloves, lots of gloves. We have eye black and icy hot and rehab boots of assorted sizes. Man, we need to have a garage sale, except now we have the grandsons!

The point is, we never sent our boys onto a court, field or mat without the proper gear for their protection and to enhance their performance. In our culture, we do a fair job of encouraging physical strength in our children, but what about spiritual strength? Are we teaching them how to "gear up" to defend themselves against the schemes and the fiery darts of the enemy?

> "Finally, be strong in the Lord and in his mighty power. Put on the full armor of God so that you can take your stand against the devil's schemes...so that when the day of evil comes, you may be able to stand your ground, and after you have done everything, to stand"
>
> Ephesians 6:10-11, 13 (NIV)

So, when the day of evil comes...not *if* it comes, but *when*...do our sons have their armor on? I love that our Great King has not left us vulnerable. If our boys will put on the armor, of course He has provided for their protection!

As moms to these young men who are developing their spiritual strength and muscles, we need to teach them how to put on the full armor and how to use each piece effectively.

To my sons and to yours, here is how you gear up and develop strength for your calling and purpose. Learn to take up the full armor of God.

Belt of Truth – Son, you have a belt of truth around your waist — truth around the very core of your being where you will gain balance. The truth of God's Word is the balance in life. It keeps you centered. Base your life and your decisions on truth, and it will keep you centered and grounded.

Breastplate of Righteousness – The Word also tells us that we are the righteousness of Christ Jesus. When the enemy looks at you, he sees the righteousness of Christ. And it is His righteousness that is a shield over your heart. He is the guard over your very lifeblood. He stands guard over your heart against His enemy. God says if you want to be a strong and valiant warrior, above all else you should guard your heart (Proverbs 4:23) because life flows from it. Hide yourself behind His righteousness.

Feet fitted with the Gospel of Peace – He has not given you a spirit of fear, but of power, love and a sound mind, and you walk in peace. His peace is the covering over your feet. It doesn't matter what circumstance you walk into; with every step your feet carry with you the gospel of His peace. You truly do walk in peace, son, and until you have peace, you don't move; you simply stand!

Shield of Faith – I love this one! When I pray this over my sons and yours each morning, I ask the Lord that when the enemy looks at us, all he will see is an enormous shield of our faith! We may not understand the battle we are in, but we do know the Victor and He is mighty to save us! Boys, you are protected by a shield of faith to thwart any attack of the enemy.

Helmet of Salvation – Your helmet of salvation covers your mind, your thoughts. When the enemy would come in to make you doubt your God or your salvation, this helmet of salvation will not only reassure you of your salvation, but will also remind you what He saved you from. I love this! I know what I am capable of, believe me! But I also know what He is able to save me from! Thank you, Jesus, for a helmet of salvation!

Sword of the Spirit – This has to be my favorite! The only offensive weapon in your armor is the Sword of the Spirit — the very Word of God! When you have your coffee in the morning and in the still of the moment you hear the gentle sound of the pages of the holy Scripture turning, your enemy hears the chilling sound of a sword leaving its sheath. And he should be very afraid, because the Word is alive and active in you!

Jake wore the same shoes and knee pads all the way through his high school wrestling career. As a matter of fact, during his senior year I stitched those knee pads after each match and prayed they would last the season. During his state championship match, the last match of his wrestling career, his shoes were literally taped together because the bottom had completely let go. But he trusted that gear. It had served him well. He had worn these pieces of gear so often they were perfectly fitted to his body.

The same is true for our sons' spiritual armor. Our sons need to be comfortable in it, they need to wear it every day, and they need to understand the purpose of each piece. This isn't like dressing up as Spiderman or Captain America. This is real life. The enemy has real arrows that can literally kill, steal and destroy. Our God wouldn't have provided us with the armor if we didn't need it. Teach your son to stretch his spiritual muscles; teach him to put on his armor.

Our sons are stronger than they realize when covered in His armor. Remember...

1) If we weren't in a real life battle, we wouldn't need armor! Don't take it lightly!

2) Each morning it is your responsibility to put on the armor the King has graciously provided you, and it is just your size!

3) The Sword of the Spirit is a highly effective weapon; learn to wield it!!

Strength is the physical power to carry out demanding tasks; emotional toughness: the necessary qualities required to deal with stressful or painful situations.

I love the way another source defines it: "The power to resist attack" (www.merriam-webster.com).

> "Love the Lord your God with all your heart and with all your soul and with all your strength."
>
> Deuteronomy 6:5 (NIV)

> "Strengthen the feeble hands, steady the knees that give way; say to those with fearful hearts, 'Be strong, do not fear, your God will come...'"
>
> Isaiah 35:3-4 (NIV)

My boys both wrestled and let me just say, wrestling is a difficult sport for this mama to watch! The training that goes into wrestling is very difficult to adequately describe. The season is extremely long, and it is an individual, full-contact sport. Mano a mano…hand to hand…and may I just say it is intense! I cannot count the number of black eyes and bloody noses my boys have had over the years, but I can tell you it has built much strength.

The Father has spoken to my heart so many times as I have watched my boys struggling in a match. Sometimes all we can do for our children is to encourage them and be there. One thing that is important to me is when my kids are in a difficult situation — be it a wrestling match, giving a public speech, trying out for a spot in the choir — I want them to see my face. I want to be a constant, steady, strong support for them. They gain strength from Brian and me. But they will see me standing by their side, not running on to the mat to "save" them.

These moments are about building up their muscles. It is an opportunity for the Lord to show them their own strength and weakness. Our sons are overcomers, but as moms, we have to allow them to overcome. Our sons simply need us to be there, to be present. Lend them our support and encouragement. Believe in their spiritual strength and ability to overcome until they can believe for themselves.

The same is true for us: God's presence is really what we need. The Word tells us that it is not by might, nor by power, but by His Spirit. His presence is the source of our strength. It takes a little struggle, a little resistance to build muscle, either physical or spiritual. When our sons find themselves in a spiritual or emotional struggle, let's support them and be there to encourage and coach but not to rescue. Allow them to flex those muscles and even to strain. Sure, they may get an occasional bloody nose or black eye, but they are developing strength of the best kind.

When our sons find themselves in a spiritual battle, coming against resistance, they will need to look for the face of the King. When their eyes lock with His, something supernatural happens. Strength.

Here are a few practical suggestions for you as a mother to help your son increase his strength.

1) Spending time each day before the Lord is imperative. First, your son will gain his strength from the Father. All relationships grow and are strengthened based on the time that's committed to the relationship. Your son needs to have a time with the Lord every day. I talk to moms about this often, and frequently the response is, "I don't feel right about forcing him to have a quiet time." My response to that is, "You require your sons to take vitamins, eat vegetables and exercise; why would you not require him to strengthen his relationship with Christ?" Remember, the goal is to guard his heart above all else. His relationship with the Lord is the only force powerful enough to guard that precious heart of his.

2) Your son needs to be in fellowship with other believers who will encourage him and challenge him to keep moving forward in his faith. He needs to be a part of a strong, Bible-believing and Bible-teaching youth group (not just shooting hoops and playing

video games). Your son needs to work those muscles: pray for the sick, pray for his peers, believe the Lord for bold requests, and ask the Lord to do great things. Remember, your son wants thrill and adventure. There is nothing more thrilling and adventurous than chasing hard after Christ with like-minded believers.

3) Have spiritual conversations with your son. Ask him what the Lord is showing him. Talk to him about what he is praying about so that you can join him and agree with him in prayer. Read the Word together and discuss the meaning of the passage or how it challenges each of you. This will do two things. First, it is good for young people, especially boys, to talk about things of value and things relating to their faith. It will strengthen him spiritually to be able to articulate what the Lord is doing and showing him. Secondly, this kind of interaction is a way for you to connect with your son on a deeper level while helping him develop the ability to communicate his faith with his bride someday.

My boys are stronger than their mother — certainly in a physical sense. I still try to work out with them simply because I love to be with them, but who are we kidding? They can outdo me every day of the week and twice on Sunday, and that makes me laugh if I can catch my breath (it does anyway). But what makes me cry is that they are stronger than I am spiritually. They pray bold prayers, and they have faith to believe Him. They are committed to sharing the gospel, winning people to Christ, and then encouraging them to grow in their faith. You want to know what will bring the sweetest, deepest, most fulfilled sleep in your life? It's this: realizing that your sons are stronger than you, in every way.

Disciple

"All scripture is breathed out by God and profitable for teaching, for reproof, for correction, and for training in righteousness, that the man of God may be complete, equipped for every good work."
2 TIMOTHY 3:16-17

This Scripture in Timothy has come to be somewhat of a life verse for me: "...that the man of God may be complete, equipped for every good work." Those few words beautifully sum up what we are working to accomplish in the hearts of the young men we are raising. We are always reminding ourselves that the goal is to guard and steward the hearts of our sons, to know them and to be known by them, and to teach them how to guard their own hearts while gently releasing them to become men.

I can't decide if we make the process too simple or too complex when we allow the goal, instead, to be about our boys "obeying the rules" or "being good." Yes, our sons should obey and, yes, they should be good. However, we want more than that. I desire for your sons and for mine to be powerful, to know who they are, to make an impact, to be the influence, and to walk in the favor of the Lord. Simply getting them to "mind," well, that isn't going to cut it.

I want you to see the definitions of two words: Discipline and disciple.

Discipline is the practice of training people to obey rules or a code of behavior, using punishment to correct disobedience.

Disciple is a personal follower of Jesus during his life, especially one of the twelve Apostles; a follower or student of a teacher, leader, or philosopher.

To discipline is to train people to obey the rules and to punish disobedience. Certainly, discipline is necessary while raising mighty men. There are times when it is necessary for us to call a foul and invoke a penalty. However, I want to be a mom to my boys and not an umpire who only calls balls and strikes. As moms who want to raise young men of influence, we have to remember that we don't want to train them to simply obey our rules; instead our desire is to disciple them.

A disciple is a follower. A disciple is a student who has a relationship with a mentor or leader and who follows the teachings of that leader. As mothers, we need to have this kind of a relationship with our boys. I didn't want Tanner and Jake to just obey my rules. I wanted them to understand why those rules were important to me. What was the motivation behind the lines we drew in the sand? The why behind the what is far more important than mindless obedience. Discipling our children is relational. We are living life with them and before them. As we walk along the way, we use teachable moments to explain why we value certain behaviors, and we are able to demonstrate for them how to worship and live self-controlled lives.

There will certainly be moments of blowing the whistle and calling a foul. If our sons start to step out of bounds or throw an illegal pitch, it is our job to call it and deal with it. Discipline is intermittent; discipling, however, happens day in and day out. It is relational and life-giving. We will enjoy each stage with them, and we will love the deep mother-son bond that we will carry.

As we consider discipling our sons, there are four very important issues for us to consider. The first is, we need to keep our word. When Jake was in the first grade, we went to a wrestling parent meeting on a Sunday afternoon at a car lot. The lot was closed but there were still cars driving through the parking lot. Jake and his buddies were having a blast running and playing all over the place. I asked him not to run through the parking lot and then said, "If you run through the parking lot again, I am going to spank you."

Just a short while later, Jake and his friends come through the front door with Jake crying and his friends quite upset as well. Jake had a cut across his neck that looked like his throat had been slit. They had been running through the parking lot and just as Jake ran past one of the huge balloons that fly high in the sky on car lots, the wind caught it and it clotheslined him. He was truly hurt, and I felt very sorry for him. I tended to his neck and when the meeting finished, we loaded up to go home.

On the ride home, I talked with him to be sure he was OK. I was kind and gentle with him. Once I knew he had stopped crying and was OK I said, "Now, son, do you know what I am going to have to do when we get home?"

"Yes, ma'am, you're going to spank me," he replied.

"Yes, I am because I told you if you ran through the parking lot again I would spank you. I want you to know, son, that I am not angry at you. I am sorry that you are hurt. But I want you to know that Mom will always, to the best of my ability, keep my word."

That was one of the most difficult spankings I ever gave one of the kids. But it was important that Jake learned that he can believe me. He can trust that I will keep my word, and I expect the same from him. As he grew up it strengthened our bond, because he did keep his word. I could believe him, and we have a very strong relationship to this day. We keep our word.

Secondly, in order to have a close bond with our sons it is important for our "yes to be yes and our no to be no." Tanner is seven years older than Jake and nine years older than Madi. When Jake and Madi came along, Tanner was already in school and very involved in sports and many other things. Brian worked nights at this point, and life was very busy for me. I would often bathe Jake and Madi around 5:00 p.m., get them ready for bed, and then off we would go to a practice or game of some kind. I was working full-time and enjoying every minute of a very active family, but to say I was overwhelmed is an understatement.

One afternoon Tanner came in and asked if he could invite a friend over. My immediate response was, "No, not tonight." As a matter of fact, at this point, my answer was basically "no, not tonight" every night. I just did not feel like I could take on one more thing. As soon as the words left my mouth, I felt like the Lord was speaking to my heart, and He said, "Why not tonight, Candy? There will be many times over the next few years when you will need to say no. When you can answer yes, do, because when you say no, it needs to count."

That moment changed my perspective. I want to say yes. It thrills me to see my sons living life to the fullest. I want them to laugh until their sides ache, to love deeply, to have compassion, to chase butterflies and jump in rain puddles. I want them to run fast, fight hard and enjoy all that life has to offer. I said "yes" a lot. I wanted to. But in the moments when the answer was no, I needed it to count. I needed it to mean something to them. If we say no, it needs to be because that is what we believe is the right answer for the situation, not simply "no" because we don't want to mess with it. Our sons will appreciate our consideration and will see the value in our responses.

Next, in the special relationship that moms have with their sons, mutual respect is critical. Jake and I have offered mother-and-son retreats for some time now, and we always ask the boys in attendance, "What is the most difficult thing about your relationship with your mom?"

Without fail, the number one answer will be, "I hate when she nags me."

You know, that thing we do when we ask them 15 times to feed the dog and take out the trash? I know you are shaking your head right now, thinking if he would do what you ask him to do the first time, you would not have to nag him! I agree. But can we also agree that the issue on both sides of this coin is that neither of us feels respected? As moms, we don't feel respected when our sons don't immediately obey. Our sons feel like we don't respect them by assuming they aren't going to do what we asked. Let's make an agreement with our sons: *I will speak and act respectfully toward you, and you will speak and act respectfully toward me.*

Let's say, for example, that you would like your son to take out the trash and feed the dog. You could say to him, "Hey son, I would like for you to take out the trash and feed the dog sometime before dinner, and we are going to eat about 6:30 p.m." Have him repeat that back to you so you are sure he understands, and then don't mention it again. If he does it, great! You didn't have to stay on him, and the goal was achieved. If he doesn't, there is no need to get frustrated or to cause a big uprising. Simply say something like, "Son, please take out the trash and feed the dog now, and you are going to go to bed 30 minutes early tonight since you didn't do what I asked." I promise this will lower the emotional level in your home and lead to more peace, but more importantly this kind of interaction will be the first step toward achieving a relationship with your son built on mutual respect.

Recently at a parenting retreat, Jake and I were ministering and a father said to me, "So you treat Jake like you respect him?" And as I thought about that, my response was, "No, I don't just treat Jake like I respect him. I *do* respect him." I respect both of my sons greatly. I respect their relationship with Christ. I respect their love for their families and their commitment to their purposes. It has been years in the making, but I truly admire and respect my sons. I can't think of two men I respect more, actually, and that is a great place to be.

Finally, as we disciple these incredible sons of ours, I think it is important to teach them to push through difficulty and win. Let me explain.

Haven't we all seen it? Friends are playing a video game in the den and one is losing. He can take it no longer and simply turns off the PlayStation. The neighborhood gang is playing a game of baseball in the back lot, and one of the boys strikes out and throws the bat on the roof, ending the game. A Saturday night family game of Skip-Bo ends abruptly when a young man gets so frustrated over the hand he has been dealt that he knocks all the cards off onto the floor. You don't lose that way, I guess. But you never really win either.

What happens when there is no reset or restart?

An increasing struggle that we see in the youth of today is a lack of self-governance and self-control. This generation is so accustomed to making a bad move on the game of the week on their iPhone and then simply starting over — refreshing or restarting. If they don't like the way that it's going, they just trash it and start a new round or, for that matter, a new game. Just dump it and start completely over.

When we live in a virtual reality, nothing is solid. Every situation, interaction, or choice can be edited. We can delete it. Or simply add a filter or bunny ears to dress it up and pretty soon, it isn't reality at all. We have learned nothing. Everyone makes a bad move or decision. We all find ourselves down on the scoreboard or in a difficult place. But what happens if we have no platform for overcoming an obstacle? Our only recourse is to simply restart. We have not had to think through our current circumstances, consider our options, make a plan and then do the hard work of "going for it."

"They went out and got into the boat, but that night they caught nothing. Just as day was breaking, Jesus

stood on the shore; yet the disciples did not know that it was Jesus. Jesus said to them, 'Children, do you have any fish?' They answered him, 'No.' He said to them, 'Cast the net on the right side of the boat, and you will find some.' So they cast it, and now they were not able to haul it in, because of the quantity of fish."

John 21:3-6

These men were professional fisherman, and that night they had caught nothing. Jesus came along and asked if they had any fish. With their reply of, "No, and oh, by the way, we have been at this ALL night," Jesus did not say, "You poor guys. Come on in and we will just restart tomorrow." Instead, He said, "Cast your nets again."

What if our sons never learn the discipline and emotional integrity of "casting their net again"? Don't simply tee up another ball and start over. Play the ball from the rough. Every shot isn't perfect. I don't win every game. I strike out. I get thrown out. I have felt down for the count. I have looked at a raging sea ahead and an approaching army coming from behind. I have felt the same hopelessness of fishing all night and catching nothing. So have you, and so should our sons. Remember, you are the teacher and he is listening; he is being discipled. Model for him casting your net again.

Amazing things happen when we cast our nets again… try again…believe again…swing again…pray again…trust again. We have a paradigm when we are faced with the same situation the next time. "Oh yeah, I've been here. Down by one in the bottom of the ninth with two outs. I may go down, but I'm going down swinging." Go for it. Push through. Overcome.

You sure don't lose your breath with tears and dirt running down your cheek as you click the restart button, but oh, the joy of seeing your Father give you the sign to swing for the fences and then, giving all you've got, "to be equipped for every good work."

PART III
Hope

Daniel

Hope – "a feeling of expectation; a desire for something to happen."

My sons and I have discussed a multitude of times that if Hollywood would make a superhero movie based on the heroes in God's Word without any embellishing, it would be the best movie ever made. The Bible is full of real-life superheroes! These heroes didn't leap small buildings in a single bound or wear capes, but they did shut the mouths of lions, call fire down from heaven, and march around the city until the walls crumbled! Now, that's a hero! Daniel makes the superhero list in my book every time.

Daniel chapter one begins: *"In the third year of the reign of Jehoiakim king of Judah, Nebuchadnezzar king of Babylon came to Jerusalem and besieged it...Then the King commanded Ashpenaz, his chief eunuch, to bring some of the people of Israel, both of the royal family and of the nobility, youths without blemish, of good appearance, and skillful in all wisdom, endowed with knowledge, understanding, learning, and competent to stand in the king's palace, and to teach them the literature and the language of the Chaldeans."* Daniel 1:1, 3-4

The Israelites were taken captive, and Daniel and his friends, the best and the brightest, were also taken. Their culture and values were hijacked, and the enemy rushed in to besiege all that they held dear. Nebuchadnezzar instructed Ashpenaz to gather the attractive, wise, knowledgeable and competent youth, so that they could stand before the king and learn the literature and language of the enemy. The purpose of this instruction was to change the way these young men perceived and interacted with the world.

The schemes of the enemy are often effective, but they don't change much. He is up to his same old tricks. Seek out the attractive, intelligent, and competent youth and train them in literature (Internet, social media, technology, articles) and language (blasphemy, vulgarity, slight untruths, flattery, prideful boasting) of the enemy. The enemy is intent on using the enlightened "new" culture to change our young people's values and perceptions and alter the way they interact with the world.

Daniel is a powerful example of being *in* the world but not *of* the world. Daniel was in the service of Babylonian kings for most of his life. He lived out his days in a foreign land that served other gods. However, Daniel's hope was in the Lord. Daniel was always expectant that the Lord would show Himself faithful, trustworthy and powerful. Daniel hoped that he would see the Lord in the land of the living. He desired it, and our God did not disappoint.

Our sons are living in a foreign land, and the enemy has attempted to take them captive. However, their hope, their expectation, must be that their God will show Himself faithful, trustworthy, and powerful.

"I do not ask that you take them out of the world; but that you keep them from the evil one. They are not of the world just as I am not of the world. Sanctify them in the truth, your word is truth. As you sent me into the world, so I have sent them into the world. And for their sake I consecrate myself, that they also may be sanctified in truth."

John 17:15–19

Our hope as mothers is that our sons will learn from Daniel some things about relationships, prayer, and adventure. Because, you see, Daniel had strong friendships with his fellow believers and with the Babylonian kings, as well. Daniel was committed to prayer and a personal interaction with the Lord. That is what quite literally landed him in the den of lions! But adventure — did he ever experience adventures! His fellow captives were thrown into a furnace and walked out not even smelling of smoke! Daniel faced the king's diet, the lion's den, dream telling, and the handwriting on the wall!! Wow, talk about adventure *and* hope in the Lord to show Himself!

But Daniel's life was not perfect — far from it, actually. It was difficult. Very difficult.

Apologies are in order. There are those rare occasions when one would just like to be gut level honest. Recently, I was having a wonderful evening and not because everything was perfect. What if I said, *everything isn't perfect; in fact, far from it?* At the time I am writing this, we are in a difficult season with our family business. My husband is stressed. I am stressed. My oldest lives 21 hours away, and that includes my three grandbabies and precious daughter-in-law. And it's 21 hours with no weather delays, mind you. Within the last 10 days, I kissed my grandbabies goodbye for the next five months. There is something seriously wrong with that.

My baby girl just graduated from high school — did you catch that? At this moment, she is only weeks away from her first apartment and her first semester as a college student. That means we are weeks, days, away from the empty nest! How did that happen?! My Jake is nine hours away knocking his junior year of college out of the park. But he is nine hours away, and I am weeks away from hugging that precious neck. Oh, yeah, I did say I was having a wonderful evening, didn't I?

Recently I received an email from a precious friend that I have not heard from since middle school. I bet I haven't seen her in 25 years — what?! She was emailing me about something very raw and personal to her, but something she said to me in the opening paragraph of her email has played itself over and over and over in my mind, "It seems like you have everything." It seems like you have everything — thus the need for that apology.

I apologize for these and many other social media posts that people (myself included) innocently and rightly post:

- For all of the vacation posts
- For the perfect report card posts
- For the beach, 40-year-old body, posts
- For the millionth dollar made in a new business venture

- For the intact, healthy family relationships for 10 generations posts
- For the graduation and going to a division 1 university posts
- For the 8,000-people saved this year posts
- For the completely healthy, gluten-free, no preservatives, home-grown diet posts
- For the homecoming queen posts
- For the my son is home on fall break posts

I do not have it all. Neither does anyone else on your Instagram feed, though we make a good show of it! I will tell you that my family has some of the same crises yours does. I don't see my grandchildren for months at a time. My baby girl is one of my best friends and will be leaving for college soon. I have crow's feet. My son at A&M is still learning the ropes, and every morning I talk myself out of driving nine hours to see him. My husband has been at this insurance thing for five years, and … well? My mom passed away much too young. I don't see my dad much these days. I love my work, but it certainly has its difficult moments. I need to lose a few pounds, and it is imperative that I make these hair appointments to take care of the gray…I mean "highlights." I don't always have my dishes or laundry done, and I am no pioneer women.

Whoa. I said it was a wonderful night, didn't I? Well, tonight Brian is quail hunting. Jake is on a weekend break in Galveston with buddies. Tanner is home from an Air Force run of several days with his bride and babies. I took a hot bath (I haven't had time for a long bath in years!), and I am home alone. I have listened to my favorite worship music, sought the Father, and decided to pen these words.

My crisis isn't your crisis, so I will spare you the details. I apologize for times that my social media posts, or anyone else's, bring you to tears. We are all just trying to make it. I know it seems that everyone's life is much easier, more prosperous, and just downright better than yours. My life is far from perfect, and I give you my sincere apologies if I have made it seem any other way.

I cried just today because there are parts of my heart that are broken. But maybe the next time we see someone else having a "perfect" life, we could have a different perspective. What if we consider that our Facebook "friends" don't have perfect lives? Most of the time, their lives are hard, stressful, emotional, overwhelming, monotonous, and messy. Maybe our friends are just trying to celebrate the good times when they happen and get through the difficult, much like we are.

As I have been home alone — well, alone with One Majestic Guest — He reminded me that He is with us. He is our Protector, our Defender, and our Friend. I am pretty blessed, as are you. Let's focus on the truth that He is enough for us all. He makes my night and my tomorrow wonderful. Let Him do the same for you.

Our sons will find hope in relationships, prayer, and adventure but not in a perfect life. We are aliens in a foreign land. Our sons will need to remind themselves of the values, literature, and language of our King and His Kingdom as they hope with expectancy to leave a lasting mark on this foreign soil.

7

Relationship

"All I ever hope to be, I owe to my angel mother."
PRESIDENT ABRAHAM LINCOLN

"I prayed for this child, and the Lord has granted me what I asked of him. So now I give him to the Lord. For his whole life he will be given over to the Lord."
1 SAMUEL 1: 27-28 (NIV)

If you are anything like me, you could not wait to be a mom. I had prayed for a family for years before Brian and I met and began this crazy journey. You may have felt the same way or you may have been completely surprised when you got the news that your precious baby was on the way. Either way, if you are the mother of a boy, your story began with that bundle of energy and love that stole your heart.

In this chapter, I would like to look at the unique, complex, and wonderful relationship that mothers share with their sons. I love the biblical story of Samuel, and frankly, my constant prayer is for a generation of Samuels. At a very young age, Samuel learned to recognize the voice of the Lord. He loved and served the Lord with an obedient heart all the days of his life. I am sure that his precious mother who prayed for him and committed him to the Lord must have had a lot to do with what a godly man he became.

Something that has always struck me about Hannah's story is that from the moment she began to ask the Lord for a son, she began releasing him back to the Father. What a paradoxical thought, nursing and learning all the details and awe contained in this male child while at the same time releasing him safely into the care of the Lord. Now Hannah had a more difficult task than most of us; she physically delivered little Samuel to the temple to serve there at a very young age. Many theologians believe that he was no more than four years old and may have been even younger. Praise the Lord that we are not facing the physical release of our boys, but we must understand that a death grip of fear around the wrist of our sons will prove to be counterproductive. From a mom's middle-of-the-night cuddles rocking her son to those precious days years later when she holds *his* children safe in her arms, the goal is a strong, healthy relationship with him.

Being a female, I always believed that I understood girls a little better. I was intimidated and a little nervous when my first two were boys. I decided fairly quickly that I needed to figure out how to relate to them and that really the obligation was mine. I was the adult, and I was the one who had to learn how to bridge the gap between painted nails and relaxing baths to jock straps and stinky gym bags. The funny thing was, I had a passionate desire to figure it out.

Something else to point out is that no two boys are formed by the same mold. If you have more than one son, don't be fooled into thinking you can relate to them in the same way. They will likely be as different as night and day.

Here is a great description of that very point from one of my dear friends:

"My relationship with each son is different. There are a lot of similarities, like they each love to watch sports, old TV shows and movies with me, but they are different in their ways of opening up. My oldest son loves to talk and has never met a stranger, so talking to him comes easy. He will tell you anything and sometimes, especially during the teenage years, he would tell me more than I wanted to know. Ha! Ha! But he is the type who is up front and honest and tells it like it is. He holds nothing back. If you don't want to know all the details, then you'd better think before you ask! He also is a very humble person and truly cares about people. He never wants to see someone hurt or struggle, even if they have wronged him in the past. He is by far the easiest son to talk to, and I don't have to work at getting him to open up. He is like the friend you have had for 50 years and even when you haven't seen each other in five years, you can pick up right where you left off.

"My younger son, however, is like starting a new friendship every day at times. You have to work at getting to know him and getting him to open up and talk so your friendship can blossom. I've always joked that the reason he is so quiet is because his older brother was always talking. The older son is also very loving and good at showing affection. He tells me all the time that he loves me and will give me a hug and a kiss anytime regardless of who is around. My younger son will answer a question with the least amount of words possible. He is not as comfortable showing affection or his emotions in front of others. He does tell me he loves me and he will give me a hug, but he is just more reserved. They are different, but I love my relationship with each boy. They are each unique!"

I can certainly relate. There are many similarities between Tanner and Jake, but there are differences even in those similarities. They are both very athletic, authentic, and relational. Both of our sons love people and have many friends. They both love music. Jake is an incredible musician, and Tanner can dance with the best of them. Both are really great big brothers to Madi. She might call Tanner to have her spirits lifted and have a good laugh, and call Jake for advice and support. Both of the boys are great communicators. Tanner is quick-witted and could be a stand-up comedian while Jake is a deep thinker and very articulate. Jake chooses his words carefully, but they are full of compassion and can pack a punch. It didn't take me long to realize that I, as their mother, needed to learn how to get into each of their worlds, individually.

We must be a part of their world.

I read a short section in the book *Wild at Heart* by John Eldredge[1] several years ago, and it absolutely changed my approach to my sons. The author discussed the importance of the approach that a mother takes with her son and how that approach shapes the relationship later in life. A main theme in the book is that every man has a battle to fight and an adventure to conquer. He desires to know that he is strong and has what it takes to be a man.

When it comes to fostering a strong, healthy relationship with your son, the very best piece of advice I have for you is *don't baby him (no matter how young he is)!* When we baby or talk down to our sons, it is emasculating to them. Have you ever heard a mother of a man in his thirties ask him if he is eating well or if his wife is making sure he is taking his allergy medicine? Imagine how embarrassing and insulting that is to the son and even to his wife. Doesn't that shed some light on the stereotypical thought that when boys marry they are often closer to the wife's family and become distant from their own? Some of that could have to do with us, their mothers. Our sons don't know how to take us, and when we are condescending to them it makes them feel weak and dishonored. If that happens many times, we'll start to hear from them less and less because it is awkward and uncomfortable.

I don't want that kind of relationship with my sons, and I am sure you don't either. I love my boys, and I know you love yours as well. I pray daily that my sons and I will remain close and that they will realize I am always in their corner. I want to do my part to ensure that they never have trouble relating to me. We raised our boys to be mighty, godly men. Let's grow a healthy relationship with them so that we get to enjoy the men they become.

If you are anything like me, you are full to the brim with nurture and love for those energetic, funny, precious boys. I had nicknames for the boys and I loved to sing songs to them. I loved to have them lay their heads in my lap and to scratch their backs. I made their meals, washed their clothes, packed their bags and left notes in their lunch boxes. I prayed for them at night and many times watched them sleep. I doctored many cuts and kissed more than my share of black eyes (thanks to wrestling). I adored my boys and still do, but I want to make things as easy for them as possible.

Our desire is for our boys to have a healthy relationship with us. Have we considered that the way we talk to them, treat them, and approach them may not aid in their journey to becoming a man? Years ago, I would have been the first mom to kiss my son goodbye in the school drop-off lane at the middle school or to yell, "Good luck, sweet boy!" at a baseball game. Or how about running out on the court or the field when they are hit with a ball or elbowed in the eye? We are simply trying to be loving moms, but have we thought about how that makes our boys feel?

They are trying to become strong young men, and our approach either encourages this process or causes them to question their masculinity and creates awkwardness between us and them. That is not the goal. Allow your son to grow into a man, and allow him to feel strong around you.

After reading *Wild at Heart* and after some encouragement from my husband, Brian, I began to understand. There's a lot I can do when my boys are young to strengthen and improve my relationship with them as they grow up. I began to ask my sons to open things for me and carry things for me (when I was capable of doing it myself). I was aware of actions and responses that might embarrass them or cause them to feel "babied." Sure, I hugged and kissed them, I was (and still am) very tender toward them, but that was usually expressed at home after the big game. I spoke to them with respect even as teenagers. I didn't shout or name call. I would never run onto the field these days if my son sprained his ankle. My sons are young men and I need to honor that.

Once when one of the boys was about eight years old, he was kneed in the nose during a baseball game. It bled so badly he had to come out of the game because the bleeding wouldn't stop. I didn't run out onto the field, though I was concerned and maybe wanted to. I kept my seat. I let him get through it. When we got home that night, he came into the kitchen and said, "Mom, that really did hurt." I was able to hug him and check his nose, to tell him how tough he was and how proud I was of him for pushing through. I was able to "mother" him without robbing him of his strength.

In no way am I suggesting that our sons should not submit, obey, or honor us. They simply must. But if I want my boys to be confident in their relationship with me, the first woman in their life, I need to show them honor and respect as well. I need to treat them as though they are strong and capable. I want my boys to relate to me their whole lives, not just when they are my little "snookums," and if that is my desire, a lot depends on me.

My relationship with the boys has gradually changed.

Tanner is married to Whitney and they have our four beautiful grandbabies. I text him often, particularly when I see something funny. He knows the best jokes and can always brighten my day. Tanner is now getting into marketing and he helps some with things related to our ministry. He loves that he is able to help and serve Hope Choice because the ministry has been such a blessing in our lives.

There have been times when Tanner has a friend who would like to talk about Scripture or may have questions related to a pregnancy or relationship he thinks I might be able to help with. He will call and we will talk about how we might serve his friend. He has a kind and compassionate heart, and he loves people. I see Tanner in his children, and he is a wonderful dad. It is a beautiful thing to watch that son of yours interact with his own children, taking some of the things he has been taught him but improving on others. I admire him and am so proud he is mine. Life is a beautiful circle.

Jake is 20 and finishing his undergraduate degree at Texas A&M. He desires to pursue a degree in medicine. He is purposeful and disciplined. He is a leader in a Christian organization on campus, teaches Sunday school for first graders at his church, and loves to go on mission trips. His faith encourages and challenges me. He is very busy. He now does his own laundry, buys his own groceries, and decides for himself how much sleep he will get each night. But we talk every day — not because it's necessary but because we want to. I enjoy hearing about his day and listening to his tone and his excitement. He will sometimes text me specific ways I can pray and occasionally he asks for help doing different things.

He checks on me too: "How are things at work, Mom? How did the banquet go last night? What's going on at the schools? How was church this week? Mom, are you doing OK?" He is my son and sometimes still needs some advice. He always needs encouragement; we all do. He even initiates hugs and will let me hold on to that sweet — I mean strong 😊— neck as long as I want. I trust him. An incredible transition has taken place: he is my friend, one of my closest, and I really like him.

Keep fighting for relationship with your son. Allow him to be strong and to grow. That doesn't mean he won't always need his mama; he most certainly will.

8

Prayer

"I remember my mother's prayers, and they have always followed me. They have clung to me all of my life."
PRESIDENT ABRAHAM LINCOLN

Wow. "My mother's prayers have clung to me all of my life." I cannot think of a more beautiful, meaningful statement a son could make about his mother. Mrs. Lincoln must have been extraordinary. Praying for, over, and with our sons might quite possibly be one of our highest callings as a mother.

Tanner was a busy, active five-year-old when Brian and I met and married. I didn't step into motherhood as a nursing mother to a newborn. I entered motherhood at the wisdom-filled age of 23 by hanging on for dear life to the bicycle seat of my very own rambunctious kindergartener. It didn't take me long to realize that prayer wasn't just an option; if I was going to do this thing anything close to "right," it was my only option!

I remember one night sitting on the edge of Tanner's bed, watching him sleep. It was a few short weeks until Brian and I were to be married, and as tears streamed down my cheeks

I prayed something like, "Father, I am blown away that You would entrust me with such a privilege. That You would allow me a portion of this incredible, precious little boy's heart is certainly more than I could ask, imagine, or deserve. Help me to always appreciate and acknowledge this gift straight from Your hands. Lord, help me to love Tanner with a mama's love and to allow him to love me in return, any way he chooses. Lord, make me wiser than my years and more compassionate and full of grace than I know how to be. I will protect him with a vengeance and will stand in the place You have created for me in his life. Thank you for his mother, Jana, and give her all the strength and support she needs to steward this young man. Help her and me to work together on this motherhood thing, and may we one day celebrate the mighty man You raised. I trust you to make me the mother Tanner needs me to be. I will be his mom, and he will be my son."

Those early days of being a mom set me on track for likely millions of hours on my knees for all of my children and certainly these two little men sleeping under our roof.

It was two short years before Jake entered our lives. As you may know, my testimony consists of an unplanned pregnancy my senior year of high school that ended in an abortion. It is easily the biggest regret of my life, but a story for another book entirely. After Brian and I married, I had two miscarriages. Jake would be my fourth pregnancy and firstborn child. Suffice it to say, that is the motherlode of maternal instinct! For this child, I had truly prayed for years. The moment this young man was born, all that "love" came gushing out like a dam had burst! It was almost too much for me, it was definitely overwhelming to his daddy, and it was more than any seven-pound bundle of boy could be expected to bear!

Something else you should know is that I am a TYPE A personality in all caps! So, I have a plan, likely including a list, for everything. The first few months of Jake's life consisted of a routine — a routine not excluding prayer time. We would pray when we woke up. Bathtime consisted of bubbles, toys, towels, children's praise songs, anointing oil, lots of lotion (which, by the way, all of my children avoid like the plague now), and prayer. The last words he heard as he drifted off to sleep were the prayers of his mama.

"Lord Jesus, make Jake into a mighty man. I ask You, Lord, to grant him favor and influence with You and with others. I ask, God, that he would be bold in his prayers, faithful in his pursuit of You, full of life and laughter and hope. Thank You that he will be a leader among leaders, and his testimony and his prayers will carry much weight. Make him a mighty man in Your kingdom, Father. Please, Lord, don't let me mess him up! Help me to be the mama that he needs, never far away emotionally, always believing he can be and do more than he can see in himself, and always listening so as to be a safe place for him. I give him to You. Make me strong enough to be his mama. He is my son."

Those are just two examples of prayer for my sons in my early years of being a mom. We have all likely heard it before, but we have certainly thought it: Parenting boys is hard.

Amidst all of the laundry, the dishes, trips to the grocery store and the doctor's office, sporting events, spelling tests, school plays, and sibling arguments, we are commissioned to raise these little people to be productive members of society who bring honor to the King. We worry about them not fitting in and we worry about them fitting in. We want them to be "different" but we don't want them to be left out. We want them to be righteous, but hip. We want them to be bold, yet obedient.

We want them to be what God has called them to be — and at some point, we feel very responsible to make that happen. What we must realize is that it is not we ourselves who can accomplish this, but it is the Holy Spirit in us.

"'Not by might, nor by power, but by my Spirit,' says the Lord of hosts."

Zechariah 4:6

I can put my finger on the moment I realized that I am really not in control of my children. When it all boils down, they make their own choices and there are few things that I can *make* them do. As parents we present the same deal to our children that God presents to us,

"I've set before you life and death, blessings and curses. Now choose life..." Deuteronomy 30:19 (NIV). And oh, how we hope they choose life!

But have you ever thought about your parenting as your sacrificial worship to the Father? When I began to view my role as a mother as an opportunity to shower my worship upon the Father, it changed my approach almost overnight. I don't make parental decisions based on trying to control my children anymore. I don't do things so that my boys won't do anything that will embarrass me. I still struggle and am certainly not operating perfectly in this new knowledge. But what I can say is that now, my parenting is about my relationship with the Father. I take very seriously the fact that He has entrusted these amazing people to Brian and me.

When we make decisions about the things they can participate in and those they can't, or when we decide the details of curfews or influences in their lives, it is truly about what the Lord would have us do. That is certainly not easy, because oftentimes, we do things differently from what some families we know do, and that is perfectly fine. But we do our very best to make decisions that glorify the Father and protect our children. I am not responsible for their choices, but I am responsible for mine. I don't want to let peer pressure or my own ego affect my children. I want them to be permanently affected by a holy God whom they seek diligently. That is success in my book.

Prayer has been the most powerful tool the Lord has granted me in the lives of these two young men. My boys love each other and share some of the same interests, but their personalities are like night and day. Tanner is fun-loving, easygoing and quite charismatic, while Jake is strong, driven, and focused. With that being said, the prayers this mom has prayed over the years have been unique to the situations and challenges they faced individually. The boundaries set for the boys, the level of supervision, the discipline, the approach we took in parenting — all have been unique to the individual boy. But the time spent on my knees in prayer for them has been a constant. As the boys have grown into men, the situations and consequences they faced certainly changed and so did my prayers. I battled for them through many, many sleepless nights. On countless occasions, face down in the hallway outside their bedroom door as they slept, I soaked the carpet clean through with my tears.

> "...The God who gives life to the dead and calls into being things that were not."
>
> Romans 4:17 (NIV)

Are you fighting for that in your prayer life, calling things that are not *yet* as though they were? Sometimes these "battles" are fought in the still of the night in the hallway, sometimes loudly as you take the ground of your house when you are alone for those few minutes before they rush in starved after practice. And sometimes these battles are fought with anointing oil and with your hand on their precious heads as you speak it out in their hearing.

When your sons hear you, in your sweet voice, do battle on their behalf and petition the King to intervene and provide — it gives them confidence to do the same. Teach your son to pray. Teach him what it means to have a genuine, personal relationship with God Himself. He hears us and He longs for a relationship with your son.

Just recently, Jake, who is currently a college junior, called simply to ask as if he could pray for me. He prayed that the Lord would bless the very words on this page. He prayed that the Lord would protect my heart and my thoughts and that no scheme of the enemy would prosper. Jake prayed for you, too. He prayed that moms would be reminded of the power the Lord has granted them to do battle on behalf of their children, their sons. He asked the Lord to renew our hope as moms that the Lord does hear and is moved by our prayers. He prayed that the Lord will be the finisher of all of our faith.

When I lathered that young man up in lotion, and spent hours talking with his Father about the kind of God-fearing young man he would become, I had no idea the power in those words. My boys have hearts for the Lord and as they are walking out their own unique callings — they are powerful.

At the very core of all those prayers and declarations, I am a mama who simply loves my sons with a kind of love that words cannot describe. But to hear that mighty young man make declarations over his mama brought me straight back to my knees. I have tears in my eyes with expectation of the day that your precious son calls to say, "Mom, can I pray for you? You taught me well." There is nothing in this life sweeter. And I am sure it sends the enemy running.

Here are a few prayers to get you started.

Self-Control

Lord, I pray that You would help our children to control themselves in their behaviors, thoughts, and motives. Lord, give them the ability to make You the highest thing in their hearts and minds and chase hard after You.

> "Similarly, encourage the young men to be self-controlled. In everything set them an example by doing what is good."
>
> Titus 2:6-7 (NIV)

Discernment

I pray, Father, that our children will be able to see truth in all situations and circumstances. I ask, Lord, that they would be able to discern when they should speak and when they should be silent; when they should flee and when they should stand for truth.

> *"I am your servant; give me discernment that I may understand your statutes."*
>
> Psalm 119:125 (NIV)

Influence and Favor

Lord, I ask that You would give our children influence and favor with their peers and teachers. I thank You, Father, that You go before and behind them and that You have ordered their steps. Lord, I ask that they not fall to peer pressure but that they would be a positive influence pointing people to You.

> *"You hem me in behind and before, and you lay your hand upon me."*
>
> Psalm 139:5 (NIV)

Strength

I ask, Father, that You would make our children strong in their minds, bodies and spirits. Lord, I ask You to give them the strength they need to stand, even if it means standing alone.

> *"It is God who arms me with strength and keeps my way secure."*
>
> Psalm 18:32 (NIV)

Passion

Lord, I ask that You would grow passion in the hearts of our children to pursue You and to desire their own intimate relationship with You. I ask, God, that You would create an unquenchable thirst in them for You and Your glory.

"Take delight in the Lord, and He will give you the desires of your heart."

Psalm 37:4 (NIV)

Submitted Hearts

Lord, I pray that You would give our children hearts that are submitted first to You, then to their parents and to authority figures. I thank You, Lord, that our children are not rebellious in Jesus' name but submitted to the calling and authorities You have placed over them.

"Children, obey your parents in everything, for this pleases the Lord."

Colossians 3:20 (NIV)

Adventure

I pray, Lord, that You would blow their minds. Father, would You take them on their own great adventure? I praise You, Lord, that a life spent seeking You is full of life and wonders. Thrill them, Father.

"May he give you the desire of your heart and make all your plans succeed. May we shout for joy over your victory and lift up our banners in the name of our God."

Psalm 20:4-5 (NIV)

Focus

I ask, God, that they would be so busy running hard after You that they would not be distracted. I thank You, Father, that You have set their feet firmly on a path and I pray that they will not turn to the right or to the left.

> *"Whether you turn to the right or to the left, your ears will hear a voice behind you, saying, 'This is the way; walk in it.'"*
>
> Isaiah 30:21 (NIV)

Good Friends

Lord, You created us to need others. I ask, God, that You would give our children good friends with hearts turned toward You. May their friends be a support and an encouragement to them in their faith. Lord, give them friends to stand with them.

> *"The righteous choose their friends carefully, but the way of the wicked leads them astray."*
>
> Proverbs 12:26 (NIV)

Hope

Lord, please grant our children hope — hope to believe that You are who You say You are. Your promises are not only true but are true for them. You are their inheritance, and it is in You that they place their hope.

> *"We wait in hope for the Lord; he is our help and our shield. In him our hearts rejoice, for we trust in his*

holy name. May your unfailing love be with us, Lord,
even as we put our hope in you."

Psalm 33:20-22 (NIV)

Moms, your prayers are a beautiful fragrance before the Lord. While writing this chapter, I listened to a sermon by Jentezen Franklin. He shared this story... keep praying.

The year was 1820, and Peter Richley was a grateful man. He had survived one of the strangest and most harrowing events known to mankind. The ship on which he had been traveling sank. He was rescued. By some strange twist of circumstance, however, he was on another ship that sank.

He was rescued again. But, again — a third ship he was on sank. He was rescued for a third time. Yet, his fourth ship of passage soon sank. And unbelievably, he was rescued for a fourth time. Then a fifth ship sank as well.

It would have been laughable had it not been so serious. On the high seas, however, he floated with the serene confidence that somehow God did not want him to die. And sure enough, as if on cue, another ship came by and answered his call for help.

This ocean liner, The City of Leeds, *was named after its British city of origin. It was bound from England to Australia and traveled the same sea lane as Peter Richley's downed ships. The crew of* The City of Leeds *hoisted Peter aboard and gave him dry clothing. The ship's doctor gave him a cursory exam, pronounced him fit, and then asked an unusual favor.*

"There's a lady on board who booked passage to Australia,"
the doctor explained. "She's looking for her son who disap-

79

peared years ago. She's dying and she's asking to see her son. She knows everybody on board and since you're the only newcomer, would you pretend to be her son?"

Peter agreed. After all, his life had now been saved for the fifth time. He followed the doctor below deck and entered into a cabin. There on a small bed lay a frail, silver-haired woman. She was obviously suffering from a very high fever. Deliriously, she was crying out, "Please, God, let me see my son before I die. I must see my son!"

The ship's doctor gently pushed the young man toward the bed. Soon, however, Peter Richley began sobbing. For lying there on that bed was the reason that he couldn't seem to die. Here was the lifeline that had kept him from drowning five times. For lying on that bed was none other than Sarah Richley — who had prayed for ten years to be reconciled to her son, Peter.

The ship's doctor stood in amazement as the young man fell down by the bed and embraced the sick woman. "I'm here, mom! I'm here. It's me!" Within days the fever had subsided and his mother awakened to find an answered prayer seated on the edge of her bed.

(This story was told by western writer Louis L'Amour in an interview he gave. It bears out the saying, "Truth is stranger than fiction." In researching the Louis L'Amour website, there were additional references that bear out this story to be absolutely true.)[1]

Adventure

"As soon as I saw you, I knew adventure was going to happen."
WINNIE THE POOH

I will never forget the moment I saw my son, Tanner, for the first time. He was five years old and such a handsome young man. He has always been witty, fun-loving, and able to keep a smile and a good attitude in difficult circumstances. Tanner is able to make friends easily anywhere he goes and does a tremendous job of "making his own fun" as my great-grandmother would say.

Fear is certainly not in Tanner's vocabulary; he is willing to try anything, and I do mean *anything*. If it makes his heart beat faster, causes his palms to sweat, and involves losing his breath, then count him in. Jake and Tanner have different personalities, for sure, but a love for adventure lies in the hearts of most boys and certainly does in those two.

> *"He has made everything beautiful in its time. Also, he has put eternity into man's heart..."*
>
> Ecclesiastes 3:11

The Lord has placed in the very heart of a young man a quest, a battle to fight, and an adventure to live. It is that thirst for thrill and adventure in his heart that brings worry and angst to the heart of his mama. In the early years, this little fella likes to climb *and* jump. He wants to ride his bike "super-fast" before he knows how to stop. He wants to wrestle the neighbor's dog and see how many shots with the BB gun Johnny can take. Then as he gets a little older he wants to be a superhero, hit the farthest, run the fastest, and conquer the newest video game. And then he wants to conquer the prettiest girl and drive the fastest car and prove to the varsity coach (and to his dad) that he can lead his team. Thrill. Adventure. Eternity.

> *"I will no longer drive out before them any of the nations Joshua left when he died. I will use them to test Israel and see whether they will keep the way of the Lord and walk in it as their ancestors did. The Lord had allowed those nations to remain; he did not drive them out at once by giving them into the hands of Joshua.* **These are the nations the Lord left to test all those Israelites who had not experienced any of the wars in Canaan (he did this only to teach warfare to the descendants of the Israelites who had not had the previous battle experience.)"**
>
> Judges 2:21 – 3:2 (NIV, emphasis mine)

Don't you love that? We have a Father who can fight all of our battles and win! We have a Father who can meet all of our needs and provide all of our desires. We have a Father who could make the path smooth and easy for us, never allowing us to stumble or requiring us to break a sweat. He could.

But He doesn't. He says things to us like, "(I) *did this only to teach warfare to the descendants of the Israelites who had not had the previous battle experience.*" Or "*My grace is sufficient for you, for my power is made perfect in weakness.*" (2 Corinthians 12:9 NIV).

I love that about our God. The fullness of life is to experience the joys and elation of the mountaintops. The fullness of life is to experience the peace, rest and leisure of the meadow. Oh, but the fullness of life is to experience the sweat on your face as you run your race with zeal and passion. The fullness of life is to weep from the depths of your soul out of compassion for hurting people. The fullness of life is to know the joy of victory; however, to know the joy of victory you must first take up your sword and fight.

You see, God could have chosen a safe life for our sons. An existence where they never got sweaty palms striking out at the plate. A childhood that didn't include skinned knees, bloody noses, and broken hearts. He could have provided them teenage years free of failure and exertion. It would have lacked adventure, sure, but we moms would sleep easier, and it would be safe.

Though we often jokingly say that is the life we would prefer, we don't mean it. We wouldn't rob our sons of adventure for anything in the world. There is nothing better than one of my sons running through the door — pouring sweat, out of breath, and thrilled to tell about the game he won, the fish he caught, or the mountain he climbed. These moments made my life adventurous, too.

Let's agree not to steal adventure from our sons. Sometimes, when you can buy them something they "want," don't. Have them work for others to earn the money for it themselves. Sometimes, when they feel sorry for themselves because someone is faster or stronger, don't take their side and bring hats to the pity party. Take them instead to the children's wing of the hospital and allow them to experience how truly blessed they are to have their health. And sometimes, when they are broken to the depths of their souls, comfort them for sure, but encourage them to pick up their own sword — our sword — His Word. Steady those little hands, wipe those tears, and point them to their battlefield.

Our God loves us too much to spare us the adventure. We need to allow our sons to be thrilled by Him.

However, adventure doesn't mean permission to be rebellious and lack self-control.

"Then the Lord said to Moses, 'Stretch out your hand toward the sky so that darkness will spread over Egypt – darkness that can be felt.'"

Exodus 10:21 (NIV)

My family experienced that last summer — the kind of darkness that can be physically felt. We were on a family vacation in Missouri, and we visited a cave. We were able to drive several miles down into the cave with a guide. There was electricity in the cave and, boy, were my daughter and I happy about that. There were beautiful structures to behold, and lots of interesting history.

At one point in the journey, the guide stopped and got out of the vehicle. He said, "Most people never experience true and absolute darkness, the complete absence of light." Yep, you guessed it — he proceeded to turn off the lights. Several miles beneath the earth's surface, completely void of light, we experienced true darkness, a darkness that could be felt. An intense weight or heaviness came over me, and I felt like I could not catch my breath. I literally had to talk myself out of a panic attack. I was afraid. It was the strangest kind of fear, too. I wasn't afraid of what could be hiding in the darkness; I was afraid of the darkness itself.

My cave experience that summer morning is the perfect description of how I feel about our culture. The fear goes much deeper than being afraid of what could be lurking in the darkness; I am afraid of the darkness itself.

I am unsure if the darkness is so intense that it lulls us to sleep or if we are simply becoming more comfortable with it and adapting to existing in its presence. But, make no mistake; it is a presence, a darkness that can be felt.

> "So Moses stretched out his hand toward the sky, and total darkness covered all Egypt for three days. No one could see anyone else or move about for three days. Yet all the Israelites had light in the places where they lived."
>
> Exodus 10:22-23 (NIV)

What I am coming to understand is that the darkness of our culture will likely become more and more devoid of light. However, it is possible even in the midst of it for the people of God, the church, to have light in the places where we live.

"The light shines in the darkness, and the darkness has not overcome it."

John 1:5

"...God is light; in him there is no darkness at all."

1 John 1:5 (NIV)

How do we shake ourselves awake to this palpable darkness in our culture? How do we teach our sons to live in the Light?

1) Stand near the Light. God is light. When facing decisions for our sons about technology, social media, dating, and boundaries, are we weighing them with the Light, with His Word? Do we pray and ask the Lord's direction before we give our eight-year-olds cell phones or send our seventh graders off on a group date to the movies? Are we spending time with the Lord? Are our sons? The Word tells us to ask for wisdom and our good Father will give it liberally. We, as the body of Christ, need to do a better job of standing near the Light.

2) Sometimes the answer should simply be, "No, that's not how we choose to live in our home." I would be a rich woman if I had a penny for every time a parent with tear-filled eyes said, "I regret ever giving my child that phone." I have yet to meet one who said, "You know, I wish I had given in and allowed my

child to date a few years earlier." Not to mention social media and apps with all of the filthy language, suggestive middle-school lip-syncing videos, inappropriate images, pornography, sexting, and bullying that happens every day right before your child's eyes. Every day. If your children have access to YouTube, Twitter, Instagram, Vine, Musical.ly, or TikTok, they see things on a daily basis that grieve the Spirit. When did we accept this idea — the idea that we have no power to stand against it? Do we feel helpless? Or do we simply not see the harm in it? I would love to know the answer, but I am afraid either would be equally as heartbreaking. Believe me, friend, there is harm in it and we are not helpless. Lulled to sleep and lazy, maybe, but not helpless.

3) *"My prayer is not that you take them out of the world but that you protect them from the evil one. They are not of the world, even as I am not of it. Sanctify them by the truth; your word is truth."* John 17:15-17. Sanctified. Set apart. Different. If your family serves the Living God, you are supposed to look different than your neighbors. Do you? As I have pondered the question, "How can we be fully awake?" I began to ask the Lord, "Why couldn't we just have a list?"

My list would look something like this...

1) No smart phones until at least 16 years old, and then no Internet.

2) No social media EVER!

3) No group dating in middle school.

4) Watch how you dress. Stop fighting the school's dress code and fight for your child's modesty.

5) If your sons have access to your phone, your device, or a device of their own, they have seen pornography. They have. (You don't have the only boy, or girl for that matter, who is the exception.) And likely they have seen it even if you do have filters.

6) You can't give teens the access code to your home WiFi.

7) You can't trust that your seven-year-old is watching Disney movies on your phone at a sibling's ball games.

8) Do you know what furries, tea bagging and yiffing is? Yeah, well, I wish I didn't either, but your teenagers likely do.

9) Stop allowing teenagers to have drinks in Styrofoam cups at school functions; it isn't always Dr. Pepper.

10) Don't be afraid to see what you see.

My list could go on for days. But here is the truth: you cannot stay ahead of this thing. My team and I spend hours each week dedicated to knowing what teens are doing, saying, and thinking, particularly with technology. It is like a rushing river; you can't be in the middle of it and stand. It would be likened to me saying, "I know heroine isn't good for my child, but what are we going to do? Everyone is using it. It is just the world we live in. I am just going to make it as safe as possible for my child to use." There is no safe way to use drugs, have sex, and use social media — especially for our children. There is no safe way to participate in sin.

"Yet all the Israelites had light in the places where they lived..."

I can't give you the foolproof list of dos and don'ts, but I do have one question. Is the Light on in your house? Your family is desperate for it — not only them but the next generation is wandering the streets in darkness they can feel. Will we turn the Light on for them?

I want to share with you some eye-opening statistics:

- Seventy percent of all Ds and Fs are given to boys.[1]
- Eighty-five percent of stimulant drugs prescribed throughout the world are prescribed to American boys.[2]
- Boys have fallen behind girls in virtually every area of education.[3]
- According to *The Demise of Guys,* one in three boys is now considered a "heavy" porn user, with the average boy watching nearly two hours of porn every week.[4]
- Some forty percent of boys will spend at least a part of their growing up years without a dad[5]
- Seventy to ninety percent of all boys leave the church in their teens and early twenties, and most will not return.[6]

And NOW, we have universities and others calling masculinity a mental disorder?

Staggering, isn't it? As the mother of two boys, I take this very seriously. There are few things in this world more special and difficult to describe than the relationship a mom has with her son. There are few things in this world more vital and powerful than the relationship a dad has with his son.

"Their children will be mighty in the land; the generation of the upright will be blessed."

Psalm 112:2 (NIV)

I know that our boys are a breed all their own. They have more energy than should be legal. They question things and have a need to understand. They explore, like Simba in *The Lion King*, wanting to know what lies beyond the borders. They climb trees and fences. They have spitting contests. Our boys test their limits and think they are invincible. They have eternity placed in their hearts and have an adventure to live. I love that I can look into the eyes of my boys and almost read their thoughts as if scrolling across a screen. Boys will be boys, and they are amazing.

However, as a culture we are failing our boys to assume that "boys will be boys" translates to "boys will be *bad* boys." I have watched over the years as adults assume that boys are rude, unruly, uncontrolled and misbehaving simply because there are three or four 14-year-old boys together in a mall or hotel lobby. We assume that boys will sleep around, drink, and smoke pot. The assumption is that simply by being teenage males, they are up to no good.

The Lord has placed within the heart of young men a desire to chase a dream, conquer, fight for justice, reach for the goal, run faster, lift more, be a superhero, and advance the Kingdom. He has placed a desire in their hearts to try and catch Him, to run hard after Him. All of this is good, powerful, beautiful and holy. All of this, without self-control, humility, and compassion will destroy them.

But should they learn to cover all the beautiful things that encompass their masculinity with self-control, humility, and compassion, we will have the perfect storm. Our young men will achieve adventure, advance the Kingdom, and have their own REAL relationship with the Father. They will change the world.

The goal is not to temper or feminize our young men; the goal is to allow His Spirit to shape their masculinity into a heart full of life, adventure and strength controlled by their 100% sold-out hearts to Him.

Boys will be boys…and I love it!

PART IV
Heart

Samson

Heart - "regarded as the center of a person's thoughts and emotions, especially love or compassion"

Oh, Samson. You simply must love him. Proverbs 4:23 (NIV) says, *"Above all else, guard your heart, for everything you do flows from it."* The English Standard Version says it this way: *"Keep your heart with all vigilance for from it flow the springs of life."* I think we may have just put our finger on one of Samson's weaknesses — guarding (or not guarding) his heart.

Above all else, guard your heart. What a powerful reminder for us moms! Above all else, *we* must guard our hearts, and we must teach our *sons* to guard theirs. Guarding our hearts can certainly mean being careful about entering into romantic relationships, and I don't want to dumb that down at all. But it means far more than that. Guarding our hearts speaks to being wise with our emotions, passions, and affections.

Samson is one of my favorites in the Word. Other favorites include Samuel and Daniel — two in a select crowd who were not perfect, but perfectly submitted to the Lord all of their days. There are examples in the Bible of people who had weaknesses and struggles, certainly, but who most days stumbled forward and always seemed to be moving toward the Lord and not away from Him. Now Samson would not make that list. Samson, in my estimation, was a bit ornery and maybe more than a bit insecure, prideful, and arrogant. But who can help but love him?

We read in Judges 13 that Samson's mother had been barren. The angel of the Lord appeared to her and told her that she would have a son, and that *"No razor shall come upon his head…and he shall begin to save Israel from the hand of the Philistines."* (vs. 5).

I love Judges 13:24-25, *"And the woman bore a son and called his name Samson. And the young man grew and the Lord blessed him, And the Spirit of the Lord began to stir in him…"*

Isn't that what we pray for these boys of ours — that the Lord would bless them and that His Spirit would stir in them? We love these boys of ours so much that sometimes our love and hope for them can almost overtake us. I have been consumed in different seasons with all of the hopes and plans I had for my two boys. They were so strong, so talented, so desired, so capable, so precious, and so ornery themselves that the possibilities were endless! I saw potential and opportunity around every corner! Not only did I pace the hallway and pray for them every night while they slept, but I had prayed for them for years before I ever laid eyes on them. They were amazing, and they were mine.

That is certainly what Samson's mother must have felt. She had longed for a child and gone without one for so many years. Then the angel of the Lord Himself not only announced that there would be a son, but also that he would "begin to save the Israelites from the hand of the Philistines"! What? Not only would she mother a son, but a deliverer?!? This child would surely bring only pride and joy all the days of his life!

Until he didn't. Samson loved women that were off-limits. He insisted on having a Philistine when his parents pleaded with him to take a wife from their people. Samson tested the limits. He touched unclean things, and he was dishonest. And yet, the Word tells us that the "Spirit of the Lord rushed upon him" over and over again. And over and over again, Samson did not guard his heart. The Lord was certainly not the "highest" thing in Samson's life. Samson toyed with people and then through his strength overcame them. He broke the rules and fulfilled his wrong desires. He lay with prostitutes, moved the city gates with his bare hands, tied foxes' tails together to destroy crops, and killed 1,000 with the jawbone of a donkey. He was a hot mess.

And he must have broken his mother's heart.

Then came Delilah. Samson, with an unprotected, arrogant heart, allowed her in and shared with her his most intimate secret — God's purpose and calling for his life. Samson's unwise heart and his disobedience landed him alone, in prison, nearly bald, blind, and completely devoid of strength.

There is a strength that mothers of sons carry. It is a strength that is hard to put into words. I have watched my boys break bones, break their noses multiple times, break windows and bicycles, break confidences and break curfew. I have seen them break their word and break His. And all of it, every single one of those things, have broken my heart. But with as much strength as His Spirit in me could muster, with love and authority in my eyes, I would wipe the blood, bandage the knees, stand them on their feet, and remind them that we can break our word, but He never breaks His.

I think what pierced my heart to the very core each time, however, was the understanding that my boys could choose to submit their will to the Lord. But if they chose not to, He would apply pressure on their pressure points until those knees finally gave way. The strength in the heart of a mother is what allows her to stay on her feet in the process and trust the Lord for His best when that boy she loves so much is being literally broken.

It happened to Samson, and I am amazed at his precious mama. But as we said, the Lord always keeps His Word.

Samson, a deliverer with no sight, hope, or strength, imprisoned and mocked by the Philistines, was finally broken.

> *"Then Samson called to the Lord and said, 'O Lord God, please remember me and please strengthen me only this once, O God, that I may be avenged on the Philistines for my two eyes...let me die with the Philistines."*
>
> Judges 16:28, 30

Samson fulfilled the calling on his life that he would begin to deliver the Israelites from the hand of the Philistines, but I bet it didn't look much like his mother had dreamed in her heart it would. Sometimes as mothers, we have to muster up the strength to grieve the loss of the dreams we had for our sons. It is good to have aspirations and hopes for these bundles of strength and life, but when His plan isn't our plan, we have to be strong enough to continue to trust Him, because His is certainly the right plan.

I want to encourage you, even in the seasons of brokenness we must be strong enough to see hope in the distance and remind ourselves that our God always keeps His Word.

"But the hair of his head began to grow again..."

Judges 16:22

Maybe you have been through or are now in a season of watching your son being broken. It is sometimes part of the crazy process. Taking that hot mess of an amazing boy and turning him into a young man on fire with passion and committed to the destiny the Lord has spoken over his life. Changing him into a young man whose heart is guarded and who now loves wisely and with strength. A heart with the Father on the throne, at the highest place in life. Now, He can work with that.

In this section, we will discuss communication, purity, and fight, with the importance of a wise heart at the very center.

"For though we live in the world, we do not wage war as the world does. The weapons we fight with are not the weapons of the world. On the contrary, they have divine power to demolish strongholds. We demolish arguments and every pretension that sets itself up against the knowledge of God, and we take captive every thought to make it obedient to Christ. And we

*will be ready to punish every act of disobedience,
once your obedience is complete."*

2 Corinthians 10:3-6 (NIV)

Moms of boys know how to fight. We do not wage war as the world does, but we do it on our knees, standing in the gap for these men of destiny. We demolish strongholds, arguments and pretensions, because our God is the highest thing in our hearts and lives. You keep fighting for your son and keep loving him, mama, because the hair on his head will begin to grow and he will fulfill his calling.

Communication

"As a mom, you have to look at how much time you're spending with your kids. There is nothing you will regret more in life – nothing – than not being present for your children."
JAMIE LEE CURTIS

Drum roll, please...this, my friends, was hands-down (with no close second) the issue most concerning to all the moms we talked with regarding their relationships with their sons. *Communication.*

Part of our problem is the simple gender gap. It is said that females use a whopping 20,000 words per day while males on average use only 7,000! We are out-talking our boys almost three to one. I know that is no surprise to any of us.

So how can we get on the same page with these boys who are so full of energy, life, strength and love...just not in quite so many words? We must be a part of their world.

"I'm the mom." If you ask my boys, they will tell you I say that more than a few times in a span of twenty-four hours. When I do, I am most often trying to get them to listen to me. But we need to allow those words to translate into our relationship on a different level. I am the mom; I am the adult.

That puts me in the driver's seat as it relates to our relationship.

I have the unique privilege of having my two sons followed by our daughter who has truly been the ribbon on top of our family. Madison is a beautiful, fun, and talkative blessing to me as a mama. When she comes in and goes out, she is talking! I can remember thousands of afternoons when Madi would use her 20,000-daily allowance of words in less than an hour, and I would tend to wander in and out of her monologues. To this day, Madison loves nothing more than coming in after school and sitting down at the bar with me. She will answer every question I have and give me a hundred more details to boot! She is easy to communicate with because she communicates in the same way I do!

It absolutely could not be more different from my relationship with the boys. Tanner is a comedian. He is fun-loving, he likes to laugh, and he likes to make others laugh. If I ever want to shoot the breeze with Tanner or let him tell the funniest thing that has happened to him this week, he is always ready to go! That's the way he rolls. Now, it is a horse of a different color if you are wanting to talk about something serious or address an issue of some kind.

Jake, on the other hand, is a bit on the serious side. I often jokingly say that he has been thirty years old all of his life. That isn't to say that Jake isn't fun — quite the opposite. He is a blast to be with, and of my three children I think he is most like me in personality. But he is a man of few words. He considers his responses, and when he speaks he means what he says.

The bottom line is, part of "being the mom" puts the ball in my court when it comes to cultivating my relationship with my children, maybe even more so with the boys. Boys are often less verbal than girls, so as the first women in their lives, it is up to us to cultivate relationship. Not only do studies show, but any mom knows instinctively, boys talk more openly when they are busy! Madison will sit down with me after school and talk through the night, but she is a girl. If I sit across from the boys, hand them some cookies and milk and start the twenty questions, they will clam up for sure. If I want to have a heart-to-heart with either of my boys, we need to be driving, taking a walk, or playing catch. Our boys will open up much more readily when their hands are active! So, get moving!

Learn to like what he likes. If he plays chess, play chess. Maybe he enjoys football, baseball, or debate. If he does, so should you. Learn to enjoy those things as well; that is learning to speak his language. Communicate. You don't have to be a superstar. Just learn enough so that he will allow you to hang out with him on his turf. That is where he feels safe to talk.

I am not great at throwing a football, but I can do it. Now, baseball playin', I'd give myself a seven on a scale of one to ten. But the simple fact is, if I can make my son comfortable, protect his dignity, and help him overcome that feeling of vulnerability, he will crack the door and let me inside. That is the goal, to become a part of the rugged and strong hearts they possess and to leave our mark as their mothers there.

Go to his events, and not only that — participate. Be a judge in the debate event or a scorekeeper at the wrestling tournament. Just having you there and involved is support to him. Plus, you will gain new understanding into his interests. I may not have always understood the rules of the game or competition, but one thing is for sure: when that man-child looked into the crowd, he would see his mama's proud grin.

Allow your son to take you on dates regularly. You will both come to love this time together, and there are so many benefits to one-on-one time. He will realize that talking to you is not as hard as he imagined. Your time together will also allow him to "practice" how he will interact on a date and will allow you to model the kind of young woman he should be interested in.

I have been on dates with both boys for decades. I have never had to say, "Son, we have fifteen minutes before we have to be home, so please open up and spill the beans." But I have also never been on a date with either son that we did not have a serious conversation about what was going on in his world. One-on-one time just brings it out of them. If we put down our devices, make eye contact, and truly listen, it is like a deep breath or a refreshing walk along the beach. They will talk when they are confident we are listening.

Journaling is a priceless way for us to communicate with our children and our boys in particular. I have a journal that goes back and forth with each of my children. I absolutely love the sentimental value these journals carry, but they are also tremendous tools in allowing our young men to share things that might be difficult for them to bring up verbally in a conversation.

Young men will say that it is difficult to talk with their mothers because their mothers will begin to give advice or finish the young man's sentences before he is able to get his complete thought verbalized. If moms do this, their sons will simply stop talking.

Writing in a journal the things that your son would like to share with you gives him the chance to complete his idea or thought before you respond. He will feel like he is heard and that you are trying to see his perspective before spouting off all the things wrong with what he is thinking or doing. Once he has made his journal entry, he will pass you the journal to make your reply in writing. Not only does this allow each of you equal time in articulating yourselves, but these journals will also become some of your greatest treasures as you are able to look back over years of conversations.

Talk whenever he is ready to talk. Often, dinner time or the car ride home from school is not his idea of the time to open up and pour out his heart. That's OK. Be ready to talk when he is, even if it is 2:00 a.m. or when you just ran your bath water. Most things will wait. Enjoy your time and communication with him when you can get it! I have sat on the front lawn with Tanner in the middle of the night. I have watched the sun rise and taken long walks with Jake to talk about the decisions he was facing or just his new favorite musical group. Priceless memories contain communication. Sometimes it's verbal but always it's a connection of the heart. Sounds so simple, right?? I know it is much easier said than done, but it is so worth our effort.

Something else we moms need to remember is that we cannot multitask our relationships.

I know the non-stop activity of a home with teenagers. There is always something to do, somewhere to be, or some-one dropping by unexpectedly. We live in a time when the message of the day is to have your teens busy and involved. I think we have gotten that message loud and clear, and may I add that I do agree with the thought behind it? Young people need to be occupied. They need to have schedules to keep and places to be. Oftentimes, their passions and the things that make them feel good about themselves like sports, choir, band, school clubs or church youth groups are what fill most of their time. All of these things are important. I just don't want to see us sacrificing our relationships in order to fill every moment with activity.

We parents are extremely busy, as well. It is easy to become lazy in our relationship with our children. Unless we are deliberate and thoughtful about ways to stay connected with our teens, we simply won't. I have watched literally hundreds of parents go through a time when they felt as though they hardly knew their teenagers. The sad fact is, they didn't. They had become complacent and had succumbed to society's pressures to allow their teens to be involved in everything. They allowed their child's "social life" to steal their own interaction with them.

That is not what God has called us to. He has not called us to have fragmented families who co-exist and whose only communication is arguments over who forgot to do the dishes or take out the trash. He has called us to love one another and to raise these young people to make a Kingdom impact.

We cannot rely on the "in season" ways of communicating. Our teens are completely consumed with their phones. A recent study found that teens spend an average of nine hours a day using social media, the Internet or technology.[1] Of that age group, 50% said that they are "addicted" to their cell phones.[2] Texting your children throughout the day may be a good way to communicate quick details; however, do not be deceived into thinking that this somehow constitutes a relationship. It simply does not.

My son, Jake, is a student at Texas A&M University, which is far more than a hop, skip, and jump from my home in Bushland. When he was preparing to head south for his freshman year, he asked me what my expectation was for communication. I said, "I need to speak to you every day. Even if it's just for a minute or two, I need to hear your voice. A mama can gain a month's worth of information in just the way you inhale when you answer the phone." And we have done just that; we have not missed a day yet for a phone call. Sure, sometimes it is a simple, "Hey mom! I am headed to calculus and then work. I am having a good day. Hope yours is too!" But it's enough so that miles on a map don't translate to distance in our relationship.

You cannot "squeeze" people in. How many of us have had something planned with our immediate family that would allow us to simply make eye contact and love on them, and at the last minute we felt guilty and decided to invite other friends or family to come along? We needed to spend time with them as well, so we tried to accomplish the old adage of killing two birds with one stone. But this kind of multitasking simply doesn't work. Your attention will be divided and your teens will be the ones neglected.

Don't feel guilty about spending time with your family. It is vital. Even something as simple as eating dinner together can enhance communication. It is so important that at the end of the day you spend time sharing together. You will have to schedule it. It will not happen unplanned, but it will be worth your effort.

Whether the topic is communication or any other aspect of the relationship, it is important to manage expectations. Moms and sons need to express what their expectation is for the relationship so that both are on the same page. I know that our sons desire to have a healthy relationship with us in much the same way we do. We just both need to commit to the process.

I would say once the boys were in middle school, I began to communicate to them how important details and information about their lives were to me. If I heard about an upcoming hunting trip or school dance from another parent before my son and I had discussed it, that was a warning sign to me that we were not communicating with each other effectively or often enough.

As the boys got older and entered high school, there were several occasions that one of them would come to me and say, "Mom, the guys and I want to drive to Tuesday's volleyball game that is three hours away."

I would usually respond with something like, "I need more information. I need you to continue to talk with me about this until I feel comfortable." This kind of interaction has happened enough times that Jake in particular will say, "Mom, is that enough detail? Do you need more words?" He is almost twenty and still asking if I need more words to feel OK. That is because over the years I have clearly stated to him how important detailed information is to me as a woman and as his mom.

If we will have this kind of deliberate interaction with our sons while they are living in our homes, it will pay off for us when they head off to college and even later in life. If you can train your son on the ways a woman needs to receive information and understanding, not only will you have a stronger relationship with your son, but your daughter-in-law will thank you someday as well.

Jesus, the Word with us and the only begotten of the Father, spent face-to-face time with twelve men. It is the inflection in one's voice, the twinkle in an eye, the quivering of a hand, or a hug and a grin that add life and value to our relationships. Do not become weary in the fight for relationship. In the end, it won't be the text messages or the social media pictures you will cherish. It will be the sweet memories of lingering.

Purity

*"I made a covenant with my eyes not to look lustfully
at a young woman."*
JOB 31:1 (NIV)

*"My son, pay attention to what I say; turn your ear to my words. Do
not let them out of your sight, keep them within your heart; for they
are life to those who find them and health to one's whole body. Above
all else, guard your heart, for everything you do flows from it. Keep
your mouth free of perversity; keep corrupt talk far from your lips. Let
your eyes look straight ahead; fix your gaze directly before you. Give
careful thought to the paths for your feet and be steadfast in all your
ways. Do not turn to the right or the left; keep your foot from evil."*
PROVERBS 4:20–27 (NIV)

*"Don't let anyone look down on you because you are young, but set an
example for the believers in speech, in conduct, in love, in faith and IN
PURITY…Be diligent in these matters; give yourself wholly to them, so
that everyone may see your progress"*
– 1 TIMOTHY 4:12, 15 (NIV, emphasis mine)

Purity is "the condition or quality of being pure; freedom from anything that debases, contaminates, or pollutes; freedom from guilt or evil; innocence; physical chastity; virginity" (www.dictionary.com).

One of my all-time favorite quotes comes from my favorite president, Ronald Reagan, "Don't be afraid to see what you see."

I live in the Panhandle of Texas, where it is fairly common to experience a thunderstorm. One thing I know about a coming storm is that there are many warning signs before the actual storm. Early in the morning, the meteorologists will begin saying that it looks like it could be an active evening. Later that afternoon, we will begin to see clouds building in the distance. Soon there will be a noticeable change in the atmosphere, the wind will kick in, we'll feel a few sprinkles, and then comes the downpour. Storms do develop, but there are many warning signs before we are in the midst of the storm.

The same is true with our sons. There are many warning signs before we find ourselves in a crisis, a storm. You may notice your son is running around with a different group of friends. His eating and sleeping habits may change. His language may worsen, meaning he is being disrespectful to you or other authority figures, or he is cursing. You might notice a dramatic shift in attitude. Don't overlook it. Address the problem while it is still just high winds and a few sprinkles rather than a full-blown F-5 tornado. In regard to our sons' purity, we need to take an active role as their moms to fight for God's very best in their hearts and minds.

The Lord has equipped you, and His Word says in James 1:5 (NIV): *"If any of you lacks wisdom, you should ask God, who gives generously to all without finding fault, and it will be given to you."* Ask for wisdom, He will be faithful to provide.

Our culture itself is in direct opposition to our children's purity. They are bombarded on every side with wrong ideas about their bodies, thoughts and speech, and certainly with relation to their sexuality and purity. The enemy has chosen an attack on purity as one of his favorite tools against our kids, particularly our boys, and we must take the battle seriously.

I want to share some disturbing statistics with you.

- One study found that 72 percent of college students — 93 percent of males and 62 percent of females — had seen porn before they turned 18, and another study found that 87 percent of college-aged men and 31 percent of college-aged women reported using pornography.[1]

- In 2016 alone, one particular website was visited 23 billion times. That's 729 people a second, or 64 million a day. That is nearly equal to the population of the United Kingdom.[2]

- Enough porn was watched in 2016 on this one website that all the data would fill 194,000,000 USB sticks. If you put the USB sticks end to end, they'd wrap all the way around the moon.[3]

- Last year alone, 91,980,225,000 videos were watched on this particular website. That works out to 12.5 videos for every person on the planet.[4]

- Also, 4,599,000,000 hours of porn were watched on the site in just one year. That's equal to 5,246 centuries.[5]

- According to research by security technology company Bitdefender, kids under the age of 10 now account for 22% of online porn consumption among the under 18 group.[6]

- A recent study conducted by the NSPCC ChildLine found that a tenth of 12- to 13-year-olds fear they may have a compulsion to pornography. That's right, a whole 10% of kids who just started 7th grade are saying they are already watching porn to the point where they are concerned and don't feel like they can stop.[7]

- In the United States in 2015, 41 percent of all high school students reported having had sexual intercourse; 46 percent of high school seniors said they were sexually active (had intercourse within the past three months).[8]

In our book, *Rescue: Raising Teens in a Drowning Culture,*[9] we address in-depth the topic of technology, social media, and porn. My goal here is not to address technology in particular, but suffice it to say, if your son has any kind of device, even if you have a filter it is very likely that he has seen porn and most likely on more than one occasion. We have to be bold enough to accept and admit that our families, our sons (or daughters), are not the exception to this attack. Once we accept that we are going to have to tackle this one, we can begin to strategize on how best to combat it.

The Father has entrusted nothing more precious to us than our children. And I can promise you, if there were ever a day when they needed to be guarded, it is now. Some days I am completely overwhelmed and I fight fear and anxiety because of the evil culture that our children must endure. On other days, I am so grateful to the Lord for allowing me a balcony seat. You know, sometimes an overlooking viewpoint allows us a bird's eye view over the entire situation. When you can see all the parties at work, oftentimes the schemes of the enemy are easy to discern. Even that statement almost brings a tear to my eye. There was a time when the enemy had to hold his cards close and "play the game," so to speak. He had to be cunning and sneaky so as not to be found out. Today, he mustn't work nearly as hard. He is blatant, unapologetic, and in our faces. And if we think he is in our faces as adults, it would blow your mind to see what he is throwing at our kids.

Guard what has been entrusted *to your* care. I won't go into the list of further statistics regarding porn, sex, drugs, drinking, or the lack of faith, conviction and morality this generation experiences. Suffice it to say, as parents, we are obligated to know the temptations our children face, and train them up in the way they should go. Arm them with the armor of God. Teach them of His marvelous works. Equip them to make an impact for the Kingdom. Teach them to guard their hearts. Help them to learn to wield their swords. At the end of the day, He has entrusted them to us. And His instruction is, guard what I have entrusted to your care.

I have seen a lot of teenage boys fight this battle, and do you want me to tell you the real definition of strength? It is a young man who has self-control and, because of his love for God, is living a pure life. That takes strength. We are raising boys to become young men who are strong, self-controlled, and able to make an impact for the Kingdom.

A mother is the first love in a boy's life. Do you ever stop to think about that as you tuck those little bundles of energy into bed at night? Or how about when your 17-year-old son comes in from a game and you have to stand on your tiptoes to reach that man-sized child? You, as his mom, are his first love. You are his example of femininity, of grace, of beauty, of nurturing, of what a wife should be — and his example of purity. What a responsibility! This thought has to be on our hearts when we choose how we dress, how we relate to men who are not our husbands, the words we speak, or the pictures we post on our social media feeds. Are we being a good example of purity in the eyes of our boys?

I want to address the issue of purity from the perspective of a mother's role with her son. I am not downplaying the role of a father in this area or any other. The role of a father in the lives of his children, sons and daughters, cannot be overstated or overemphasized. The role of a dad in the life of his children is arguably the most influential relationship in anyone's life. As it relates to purity, a father's role is to be someone a son can look up to and imitate. A dad is walking ahead of his son as an example of a self-controlled, pure life. You, as his mother, are walking beside your son. You are playing the role of his counterpart — the feminine side of this balanced equation of purity. As your son seeks to follow in the steps of his father related to purity, he will glance your way, mom, to validate that he's moving in the right direction. He will notice your responses and your nods of approval or your gentle redirection. The roles moms and dads play with their sons are different related to purity, but both are very important.

"I appeal to you therefore, brothers, by the mercies of God to present your bodies as a living sacrifice, holy and acceptable to God, which is your spiritu-

al worship. Do not be conformed to this world, but be transformed by the renewal of your mind, that by testing you may discern what is the will of God, what is good and acceptable and perfect."

Romans 12:1-2

In order to be pure in our thoughts as mothers, we must renew *our* minds. In 1 Corinthians 10:5 we are instructed to take every thought captive unto the obedience of Christ. In 1 Corinthians 2:16 we are told that if we are Christians, we have the mind of Christ. Before we can tackle impure thoughts and taking thoughts captive with our boys, we have to take control of our own wayward thoughts. Every thought that comes into our minds needs to obey our King. If I think a hate-filled thought about a person, if fear or anger or judgment comes into my mind — then, if I am going to live with purity, I must take those thoughts captive.

My daughter, Madi, shared with me something her youth pastor's wife pointed out to her. Madi was struggling with distraction during a worship service. She was visiting with this amazing, godly woman who said, "Imagine that distraction as a figure that is leashed and you are holding the leash. Tell it to bow down to Christ." Taking your thoughts captive is as easy as that. You have the mind of Christ. You are holding the leash. Tell your fear, distraction, anger, judgment, and even lust, to bow down to the authority of Christ. All of our lessons in regard to our boys are caught, not taught. If we are going to communicate with our sons about the authority and responsibility they have to control their thoughts, they need to see us modeling that for them. Our platform with our boys comes from a place of relationship. If all we offer them is a list of don'ts, we aren't going to get very far. **Your relationship with your son is what gains you entrance into his world and access to his heart.**

I asked both of my boys this question, "What have we done to ensure that our relationship is strong?" Jake's response was, "We have always been committed to communicate. You didn't smother me and you always listened to what I had to say. You pushed me to be the best I could be. We would talk about everything and when there was a problem, we would talk it out. We always made sure we didn't get too busy to spend time together." I can tell you it is from this platform that he and I have had many difficult, important, and deep conversations about purity. My relationship with Jake allowed me in and gave me access to speak to the deep things of his heart — and it caused him to receive it.

Something I have said to my sons and countless other young men is, "*When* (not if) you see an image of a naked girl, you will want to look. God made you to be captivated and motivated by the beauty of women. You are not bad or perverted because you are drawn by sexual attraction. God created us, and He created sex and calls it good. His intent is that a man be intrigued and enticed by his wife. That desire is a gift in marriage." When a man and his wife become one, we see the complete picture of our God (Mark 10:6-9). It is no wonder that the enemy sees the power in the intimacy between man and wife and he hates it. Satan has unleashed his most intense attack on sexual intimacy intended for marriage.

"Drink water from your own cistern, flowing water from your own well. Should your springs be scattered

abroad, streams of water in the streets? Let them be for yourself alone and not for strangers with you. Let your fountain be blessed, and rejoice in the wife of your youth, a lovely deer, a graceful doe. Let her breasts fill you at all times with delight; be intoxicated always in her love."

Proverbs 5:15–19

God is not a prude, and He thinks that sex between a husband and his bride is beautiful, powerful and good. Sex and the need for respect and honor are the three biggest needs of a man, says Jimmy Evans, president and CEO of *MarriageToday*.[10] If the enemy can destroy purity in the heart and lives of young men of God, he has dealt a severe blow to their ability to be effective for the Kingdom. I am blessed to work with young people, teens, and families as a part of my daily life. I will say, hands down, the most difficult issue facing families today is addiction to pornography. Men, women, pastors, teachers, coaches, teenagers, children, boys, girls, believers, and non-believers are struggling to overcome the intense temptation of a cheap counterfeit of one of the most powerful and intimate gifts the Father has given us. Sadly, it is so common that the temptation is to normalize and accept it, to believe that this is just the way guys are. We cannot lower the bar on this one in our homes. If someone stumbles, we help them up, dust them off, and we try again. We keep getting up. But we do not justify, accept, and normalize sinful behavior. We want God's very best for our sons.

As moms, the most difficult thing in dealing with the issue of purity in our sons may be to admit that this is a temptation for them and likely the most intense temptation in their teen and young adult lives. I know this isn't pleasant to think about, but your son *has* seen pornography. He hears other young men talk about sex, porn and self-gratification. He does. Once we are realistic about what we are dealing with, then we can get our warrior-princess armor on and go to work. **But for the love of the heart of your sons, let's open our eyes to the battle around us and fight!**

The very first thing you can do as a mother standing with and fighting for her family is to pray.

I will stand my post next to you, but we must begin to come out of the fog and see things for what they are. The battle is real.

1) Pray that our teens will be pure in their thoughts. A very important lesson for Christians to learn is how to take their thoughts captive. Each of our actions begins with a thought, whether good or bad. Let's pray that we can effectively teach our young people how to take authority over their wrong thoughts and replace them with thoughts that honor Christ.

Romans 12:1-2; 2 Corinthians 10:5;
1 Corinthians 2:16

2) Pray for purity in their hearts and emotions. I am so thankful that the Lord has given them the power to control themselves, and that when their hormones want to act up, they have authority to stand against them! Pray for control over their emotions so they can be alert and steadfast, ready in all situations. We are not governed by our emotions but by the Spirit of the Living God.

Jeremiah 17:9; 2 Timothy 1:7

3) Pray for purity with their bodies. Pray for purity in that they will wait for sexual activity until marriage.

1 Corinthians 6:19-20

4) Pray that if our sons are struggling in the area of purity, it will be brought into the light.

Secondly, we need to give our young men weapons and tactics for the battle for purity.

Communicate with your son that the enemy uses pornography against him. It is a trap. Tell your son, "When you see it, I want your first thought to be, 'This is an attack, a trap, and I need to run!'"

1 Corinthians 6:18 – Flee!

You can do that through:

- Prayer
- Praise
- Getting up, going outside and getting active; don't isolate
- Scripture

Then you need to tell your dad or a trusted male role model. We all need to be accountable. The enemy does his best work in the dark. The first step to overcome him is to bring failures and struggles into the light and bring trusted, godly men into the battle with you.

I want to encourage you that sex is still reserved for marriage and yes, there are young men who choose to abstain from sex until marriage (1 Corinthians 6:19-20). I will also say that simply not having sexual intercourse until saying "I do" is not the goal. The goal is to live a pure life. Purity is far more than abstaining from sex. Purity is the way we think, the way we feel and the way we choose to behave. We have to be wise as mothers and help our sons set boundaries of protection in their relationships.

I don't care how wonderful your son is, he is a boy and he will have to learn to take his thoughts and desires captive. He needs your help, prayers, and encouragement. You and your husband with your son will need to set clear boundaries when it comes to his dating relationships — things like: no serious dating relationships in high school, no girls alone with you in your vehicle, you can't be at our house or her house without parents being home, etc. This is between you, his dad, your son and the Lord, but boundaries need to be determined and then you all need to agree to accountability. Check in with him. Oftentimes I have asked both of my sons, "How are you doing? How can I be praying for you? Are you guarding what you see? What is the Lord saying to you? Do you have a good group of friends around you?" Again, I am able to do that because we have established and fostered this kind of relationship, communication and accountability for many years. By the way, my sons can ask the same questions of me. Relationship is paramount.

"Above all else, guard your heart, for everything you do flows from it."

Proverbs 4:23 (NIV)

It all boils down to protecting hearts. This Scripture has been one that I have prayed over all of my children almost daily for their entire lives. Guard your heart, because everything you do flows from it. The goal is that our sons' hearts be healthy, whole and alive so that all of their relationships will receive life from it. If they do not take seriously the importance of living a pure life, if they allow the enemy a foothold in their thoughts and if they allow themselves to experience sexual intimacy in any environment other than the one established by the Father, they will have a wounded heart.

Purity is not easy. It is hard work that requires commitment, persistence, strength and faith. I know enough about my young men to know that it is the hard things they have battled through that mean the most to them.

Both of my sons are wrestlers and both very successful at the sport. I have watched them face fierce opponents, fight hard for three periods and, win or lose, feel great satisfaction in the fact that they did not give up and they gave it all they had. Wrestling is a sport that requires discipline, self-control, and strength. One important part of this particular sport is maintaining the proper weight. This was the area, as a mom, that I was most involved in. Jake's junior and senior year of high school were the years we had to be most intentional with maintaining. I would prepare the meals each night. I would pack his lunch every day. I would prepare all he would eat on the day of weigh-ins and then for the tournament the following day. My husband, Brian, has always been just a great wrestling coach. He was the boys' club coach for many years when they were younger and the most helpful to them in high school. He was up with them early many mornings doing that extra workout or going over certain moves. Our entire family — little sister, aunts, uncles, cousins, and grandparents — were all at each match to cheer them on. We all had a part to play. But it was up to the boys to step on the mat. To face that opponent. To put all that they had learned into practice. To execute.

I remember both boys' last match and, man, was it emotional. Jake's was most recent. Jake had more second place finishes at the state level than was fair. His senior year was actually his 14th year to wrestle. He worked extremely hard. He overcame many injuries — pulled muscles, broken thumbs, broken noses, and even a fractured neck. He fought hard. His senior year was the culmination of it all. He enjoyed that last season focused on gaining all he could from it, not only physically but spiritually as well.

I will never forget looking down on a wrestling mat for the last time. It was at the state championship, and Jake was facing an incredible opponent, another senior who had gone undefeated for the year. I should have been so nervous, but you know, I wasn't. I had faith in his strength. Faith in his determination. Faith in his heart. He was a warrior who understood power, love, and self-discipline. He was born for moments like this.

The battle for the heart of your son is much like my wrestling story. We all have a role to play. But it is up to them to prepare themselves, to face an adversary, to fight with all they have, to remember the preparation, to lean on the cheers from the stands. They were born for moments like that.

I have prayed Proverbs 4:23 over my sons thousands of times, but mamas, this one is for us.

"Rejoice in the Lord always. I will say it again: Rejoice! Let your gentleness be evident to all. The Lord

is near. **Do not be anxious about anything,** *but in every situation, by prayer and petition, with thanksgiving, present your requests to God. And the* **peace of God, which transcends all understanding, will guard your hearts and minds in Christ Jesus."**

Philippians 4:4-7 (NIV, emphasis mine)

Do not be anxious about the giants your son will face, but pray for him. I have worn out the carpet in the hallway of my kids' rooms, and there are tear stains from one end to the other — but the peace of God is what will guard this mom's heart and mind, and He will do it for you, too. There's nothing better than seeing that boy's hand raised in victory, and I am believing for nothing less than a win when it comes to his purity!

P.S. He won. (Jake Gibbs, Boys Wrestling Texas State Champion 2016-2017 www.uiltexas.org)

Fight

*"For though we live in the world, we do not wage war as the world
does. The weapons we fight with are not the weapons of the world.
On the contrary, they have divine power to demolish strongholds. We
demolish arguments and every pretension that sets itself up against
the knowledge of God, and we take captive every thought to make it
obedient to Christ."*
2 CORINTHIANS 10:3-5 (NIV)

My Bible literally falls open to the page containing this verse — a life preserver that I have clung to more sleepless nights than I can count. *The weapons we fight with...have divine power to demolish strongholds.* As women and leaders, we can become desperate for weapons effective in tearing down the strongholds the culture would inflict upon our churches, families, and those we minister to in the outside world. These strongholds can attack our faith, relationships, and even our very peace. With wave after wave crashing down on us, we must have a weapon, a life preserver, to take hold of to help us weather the onslaught of the enemy.

"We demolish arguments and every pretension that sets itself up against the knowledge of God." Aren't we thankful that we have been given a weapon to demolish arguments and

pretensions that set themselves up against our God? On almost a daily basis, we see posts on social media, comments made by celebrities, or advertisements that mock God and all that He represents. We are encouraged to set "heroes" in a higher place than God. We are taught to put our own desires above His. Our culture indoctrinates us to consider ourselves before anyone else. We are told that we are the center of the universe and should do whatever makes us happy. *What if we, our children, or women around us make the wrong choice? Do the wrong thing? Hang with the wrong people? What if no likes me? Or what if everyone does?* All these thoughts are arguments and pretensions that set themselves up against the Lord's very words, *"For I know the plans I have for you, declares the Lord, plans to prosper you and not to harm you, plans to give you hope and a future."* Jeremiah 29:11 (NIV)

I can vividly remember a certain morning I spent with the Father, and there was nothing pretty about it. For hours I was on my face, sobbing and bargaining with Him. I begged Him to change things with one of my sons. I repented of every sin and shortcoming I could recall. I promised to do anything He asked of me. I whispered and shouted. I cried and prayed.

And when I had cried that thing through and my entire being was completely exhausted — I listened. He whispered, in His all-too-familiar fashion, to my heart, "This is not about you having control. You are not in control of your boys, and any thought to the contrary is a mirage. I am also not interested in your begging and empty promises. This is about *My promises* and your willingness to have enough faith to believe them."

It was then that I began to realize that the only course of action that would have any impact lay in *how* I related to my Father. He calms the storms and makes the winds and the waves still. I needed only to believe in the power and restoration which He promised.

Tanner is an incredible young man. He is now a husband and father of four of the most darling little ones you have ever laid your eyes on. Tanner is the kind of person that everyone loves, and I mean *everyone*. Tanner has a charisma that is unmatched, and his peers — as well as people older and younger — are all drawn in. Tan makes life enjoyable and makes others happy by just being around him. He and I, from the time the Lord brought us together, have adored one another. We have danced together, laughed a ton, cried some too, confided in one another, fought with one another, believed in each other, and doubted each other; but we have always loved each other.

Relationally, Tanner and I really struggled during his high school years. But no matter how difficult things got, Tanner did not give up on me and I did not give up on him. When I say I fought the fight through tears and intense battle for this one, it is not an overstatement. There were days I thought for sure I was watching him walk straight into a desert that would take more than 40 years to see his way through. And yet we fight, and we hope.

Tanner is now an airman in the United States Air Force, serving as a staff sergeant.. He has influence with his peers, and his little family is well taken care of and loved by that mighty young man. When I asked Tanner what he had learned from me, his answer was, "Though you were a little stricter than Dad, you were a great mom to me. I never thought of you as a stepmom. I learned how to adapt my parenting for my children from you, and you were always understanding of me growing up. I learned social skills and how to relate to people from you. You listen to others. I have watched you not change who you are but interact with those who think differently than you do and make them feel comfortable."

As I type these words, I can see Tanner and myself both filthy, bloody and spent from years of intense fighting for our relationship. One of the most precious moments of my life was at the wedding of Tanner and Whitney. At the reception, as Tanner danced with his mother, Jana, I shed a tear (or two) of joy watching the love they share. And then, catching me completely by surprise, Tanner invited me to dance to a different song, *God Gave Me You* by Blake Shelton. A few lyrics to that song are: "God gave me you for the ups and downs. God gave me you for the days of doubt. For when I think I've lost my way, there are no words left here to say. It's true; God gave me you."

If I could, I wonder if I would go back a few years to that scared, over-her-head mama or that restless, uncertain teenage boy and whisper to them the outcome of the battle? I wouldn't. I wouldn't for a moment rob them of watching the hand of the Lord work in and through them. It was all worth it, son. We won.

My God calms my storm. He stills the waves for me. This is true for our children as well, when they are being attacked by the enemy—He knows their storm, and He stills their waves. When I relate to the Father in the way I'm intended to, He is able to work through me to minister to those around me. It isn't my battle to win. It's my battle to fight with the weapon He has placed in my hands—His very Word. He will win the war.

Another gripping thought that comes to my mind, however, is that if you are the mother of a son, you are also called to equip *him* to be a warrior in the Kingdom. I can remember both of my boys running around in diapers or shorts, armed with a plastic sword intent on finding a dragon to slay. What a funny sight to see such little heroes, with milk mustaches from breakfast, set on such a valiant mission.

It can seem much the same as we raise these young men to wield their spiritual swords. Doesn't it bring a grin to our faces to imagine our three-, six-, or 14-year-olds doing spiritual battle? In Ephesians chapter 6, we are reminded first of all that the battle belongs to the Lord and that we are to be strong in His mighty power. Then in verse 11, the Lord reminds us that we have an adversary: *"Put on the full armor of God so that you can take your stand against the devil's schemes"* (Ephesians 6:11 NIV). It is our temptation to think that the enemy would allow our sons to grow up and prepare before he would launch a full-on attack against the weakest among us. But, if that is our conclusion, we would be wrong. The enemy has launched an attack against our children and he is ruthless in his efforts. Our children are faced with bullying, drugs, sex, social media, sickness, and distracted adults far too early in their lives.

I am by nature a fixer. I am most at peace when everyone is in a good place — no struggle, no obstacles, no battles. Often, I still take a deep breath and a step back to process when I want with every motherly instinct in me to intervene and "help" one of my sons in his battle. I am flooded with examples I could share in this regard.

Tanner started a new school in the second grade. He moved from a Christian school to a new district that Brian had carefully considered and selected for our family. We were in the process of building our house when Tanner began the school year. This school is in a small community where many of the kids had known each other and attended school together since preschool. Well, as is common, being the new kid isn't easy. There were about four boys who gave Tan a very hard time. They wouldn't allow him to play with them at recess. They made fun of him in the lunchroom, and they ostracized other boys who tried to include Tanner. This went on for months.

We would talk with Tanner every night about the day's events, and Brian would give Tanner good ideas of ways to handle the situation. I managed to stay calm for a while, but after weeks, this was getting completely out of control. I wanted nothing more than to make a trip to the school to handle the situation. But Brian knew best. We might be able to stop the bullying in the short term, but Tanner had to fight this battle on his own. We could give him the "weapons" he would need, which consisted of ideas and lots of Scripture, and we could teach him to use them. But in the end, it was his battle to fight and he needed to learn to use the weapons of his warfare. Eventually, these boys became lifelong friends. Brian and I even grew to love them, albeit, though I have forgiven, I haven't forgotten 😊.

It is imperative that we mothers realize that we must arm our children for the spiritual battles that they will face.

The good news is that they are equipped by the power of His might. In Ephesians 6, we learn of the full armor of God: the helmet of salvation, the breastplate of righteousness, feet ready with the gospel of peace, the belt of truth, the shield of faith, and the sole weapon of offense — the sword of the Spirit that is the Word of God!

Do we as godly mothers realize that we are quite literally training our boys to fight? To arm themselves for battle and wield a sword? Do you realize that you are responsible to teach them to be warriors? I know how you feel about that boy of yours. I feel the same about mine. I would take on a lion and bear with my bare hands if it meant that my son wouldn't have to — that's what a mama does. But there will be many days that I won't be there and, truth be told, even at this point, certainly one (and prayerfully both) of my boys is more astute in spiritual warfare than their mama ever was. But I will tell you one thing: if I am going to send a Gibbs boy onto the spiritual battlefield to face an enemy who wants nothing more than his destruction, then this mom will be the one who makes sure that his helmet is custom fit, that there is no gap in his armor, that his feet are covered in peace, and that his shield of faith is big enough to cover him. Most importantly, I will make sure that his sword is sharp and that he is proficient with it. If my son must go into battle, he will be prepared and armored. His mother will make sure of it.

Here is a statistic that might surprise you:

- A nationwide study found that only 3% of teens read their Bibles daily, and only 11% read their Bibles once a week[1]

"...Man shall not live by bread alone, but on every word that comes from the mouth of God."

Matthew 4:4 (NIV)

"For the Word of God is alive and active...it judges the thoughts and attitudes of the heart."

Hebrews 4:12 (NIV)

That would explain why we have malnourished young people and few who see evidence of God's profound action in their lives.

The sword of the Spirit, the Word of God, is our only weapon, the only weapon of our spiritual warfare that we can train our sons to wield. We must remind ourselves that it is more than sufficient, and we'd better get to the work of using it.

Here are a few ideas for training your mighty warrior to be more proficient in wielding his own sword:

- **Be a good mentor.** Spend time studying the Word yourself. Use down times to discuss with your kids the things that the Lord is showing you in your personal quiet time. Ask them for their thoughts and opinions and ask them what the Lord has been showing them.

- **Post Scripture around your home.** As a child, I memorized the 23rd Psalm because it hung on the wall in our restroom. Be creative and post His words throughout your home. Your children will memorize them with little to no effort, just because the words are familiar.

- **Look for a devotional book that would be good for your child.** I have seen some for athletes, for girls, for guys, and on topics such as depression, going deeper in the faith, etc. You know your son. Developing the habit is what is of importance. Drinking water is a perfect illustration of this. If a person has been a soft drink addict for a long period of time and then decides to drink water instead, it will be difficult in the beginning but the more water one drinks, the more one craves. It is true with the Word. Once a habit is established, the desire will follow. It will become life to them!

- **Spend time as a family reading the Bible.** Breakfast is a great time to be together for 10 -15 minutes as you start your day, feeding your children with His Word and teaching them to use their sword.

- **Have them journal.** It will help them to make sense of what they read and what the Lord is speaking to them if they put it in their own words and on paper. They can go back and remind themselves of those things the Lord has shown them in His Word and spoken to their hearts.

Our little boy in a diaper, but full of confidence in his plastic sword, may have a difficult time defeating his dragon. But take that same little boy, armed with the sword of the Spirit, the Word of God, and I guarantee you that when the enemy looks at him, he does not see a milk mustache and pull-ups. He sees a true, valiant warrior.

I want to close with a story about my son, Jake. To give you a bit of the background story, our family is no stranger to warriors with battles to fight. Tanner began wrestling at the age of five, and Jake was only four when he began his wrestling career. Jake would leave every tournament by buckling into his car seat! Both boys were very gifted wrestlers, but if you are a wrestling family, you will understand my next statement. There is absolutely no other sport like wrestling. Jake wrestled for 15 seasons. He was blessed to have 10 **second**-place medals from club wrestling state tournaments. As he entered his Texas high school wrestling career in his freshman year, he didn't make it out of the regional tournament. His sophomore year, Jake finished 5th in the state tournament and that was a tremendous accomplishment.

What I watched in my son was his commitment to the process and his coaches. He trained hard. He was disciplined, and he did not make excuses. He pushed himself to continue when he felt like he could not. We prayed. We prayed that the Lord would use wrestling to give him a platform to share the gospel. And we prayed that he would achieve a state championship, to give glory to the Father. Here Jake will pick up the story in his own words.

In the summer before my junior year, I attended a wrestling camp at Western Colorado State University, well-known throughout the country with hundreds of high school wrestlers in attendance every year. At the camp, wrestlers have the opportunity to wrestle in the neighborhood of twenty-five matches against some of the best wrestlers in the country. The camp is only four days long, so each wrestler has many matches in a short period of time. It is extremely physically challenging.

On the third day of the camp, I was blessed to be undefeated at that point, 13-0. During my 14th match, I was winning and there were only thirty seconds left in the match. I fractured my neck and tore some ligaments. For about 12 minutes, I could not move my arms and hands; I was in extreme pain. My coach and I decided to go to the chiropractor to get my neck checked out, and the chiropractor did not think it was a serious injury so he adjusted my neck. This was the worst pain I have ever experienced in my life. When we came home from the camp, I went to another doctor and had an MRI and X-rays done. The doctors discovered the fracture and the torn ligaments. The doctors told me that I would never be able to play football again, and I would not be able to wrestle my junior year.

When I left that office, I was devastated. I was extremely upset about not being able to play football, but the much bigger blow was not being able to wrestle. I asked the doctor if I could have another exam before wrestling season to see if I had a chance to wrestle. The doctor approved and gave me strict orders not to do any physical activity for six months, not even jogging and no lifting anything heavier than ten pounds. That football season was very hard for me because I could not work out at all and I watched all of my friends get to play football in my stead. I love to work out. I believe that God has given me an athletic ability for a reason, and every time I am exercising, I feel like I am glorifying Him. It was hard for me not to do anything physical at all, but I knew that the Lord had a plan for me and that my identity is in Christ and not in sports. I did battle spiritually. I prayed, memorized Scripture, and pressed in to my relationship with the Lord.

I did not participate for six months and then returned to the doctor. The doctor was amazed at the healing progress my neck had made and said he would permit me to wrestle. I was thrilled. There was no other explanation to my recovery other than the Lord's healing. I knew the Lord had a plan for me, and He revealed some of it to me that day. During the wrestling season my junior year, I felt privileged just to be able to participate. I did not take any of it for granted.

The Lord was with me, and I advanced to the Texas State Tournament. The best wrestlers from around the state were entering the gates like ancient gladiators. A little boy's dream leaped into my mind, bringing with it excitement and restlessness. When I walked through those doors, I knew that the next 24 hours were going to be unforgettable—and I was right. I will not forget this particular tournament because I grew in assurance of myself and God.

I knew the Lord had prepared me for this moment. I won my first match and was feeling very confident. All season long, we had not worried about my neck or reinjuring it. The thought really hadn't crossed our minds. I was feeling very strong and began my second match of the tournament. Only a minute or so into the match, I felt that all-too-familiar pain. I had reinjured my neck. I was devastated but tried to remain focused on the match. Through the strength of the Lord I was able to quickly win the match by pin. But I thought my wrestling career was over. I didn't want to say anything to anyone about it because I wanted so badly to continue.

My mom noticed and she asked me about it. I couldn't hold my emotion back as I admitted that I had severely injured my neck again. We called our friend, my orthopedic surgeon and his advice was to carry on as long as I could, knowing that this would be the last athletic competition of my high school career. My mom and I went out into the hall and prayed. We asked the Lord to heal my neck and gain glory through it. My mom *hugged me and I headed to prepare for my next match. I think mom and I both thought the same thing: this was likely my last match ever.*

The miracle happened during my warm-up. The Lord completely healed my neck. I lost the next match 2-1, but I competed with a healed neck, finished the tournament healthy, placing third. I cannot describe the feeling of accomplishment that I felt. I had to leave the coliseum, because I lost control of my emotions and started to cry. I knew the Lord had given me favor and I knew that I had done everything I could to bring Him glory.

I learned many different lessons from the tournament and my healed injury. Never give up, push through the pain, you are never out of the fight, trust in God, and the Lord is always with you; these are just a few truths I took out of this experience. God answered my prayers. I asked Him to help me bring Him glory and He gave me an awe-inspiring story to tell. Through that landmark moment in my life, I will never forget my experience on the wrestling mat. But most importantly, I will never forget the miracle God performed just because of His love for me.

I cannot describe what it was like for this mama to watch Jake face this giant in his life. All I could do was pray and watch as my son, with his armor firmly in place, walked out on to his own battlefield and stood. The Lord fought for him. His senior wrestling season couldn't have been more beautiful if his Father had allowed his mom to write it. Jake kept his focus on the Lord, saw several of his teammates accept Christ, and defeated an undefeated wrestler for the State Championship. The last match of his career was a win, and he was the best wrestler in the state. At the conclusion of the match, as his hand was raised, Jake pointed straight to the Father...*not by might, nor by power, but by my Spirit, says the Lord.*

Fight. And teach that boy to fight, as well.

PART V
Honor

14

Joshua

Honor – "to regard with great respect; to fulfill or to keep"

I love the Old Testament. Now don't get me wrong, I so enjoy hearing the disciples recount their experiences with Christ, and it moves me to read about all that they accomplished after Christ's return to His heavenly throne. I have great admiration for all of their sacrifice, and I am challenged in my own life.

I remember spending thousands of Sunday mornings in Sunday school with my most treasured friends, learning about Moses, Joseph, David, Daniel, and Abraham. I love hearing about Abraham, who had faith enough to believe in the one true God and to follow Him into a land that was not his own. Wow.

I love to read the stories of those on the front side of the New Covenant because it brings me such comfort and confirmation in my own life as one who is "believing without seeing" on the back side of the New Covenant. To study those who had to set their gaze forward to catch a glimpse of Him in their spirit encourages us as we use the eyes of our hearts as well to see Him coming our way.

Joshua must be one of my favorites for many reasons. He was a warrior in the faith, and from the writings regarding Joshua, I believe that sometimes he "did it scared" as do so many of us. He had some big shoes to fill — I mean Moses, are you kidding me? If you have ever felt inadequate in any role or position, thinking you couldn't possibly live up to those who had preceded you, then you have Joshua to turn to. Moses was so influential with the Israelites that God Himself buried Moses (Deuteronomy 34:6) so that the Israelites wouldn't turn his graveside into a shrine. That's the guy Joshua had to succeed. What a calling!

> *"Thus the Lord used to speak to Moses face to face, as a man speaks to his friend. When Moses turned again into the camp, his assistant Joshua the son of Nun, a young man, would not depart from the tent."*
>
> Exodus 33:11

I chose Joshua for the final section of the book because of his commitment to honor. He not only honored Moses, but most importantly, Joshua was a man who feared and honored God. He understood the concept of "regarding with great respect" Moses and his family. He was committed to fulfill his calling.

Joshua has so much to offer our sons. He was Moses's assistant. He was the son of Nun. And he was a warrior. He knew how to wield his sword.

> *"My prayer is; not that you take them out of the world but that you protect them from the evil one. They are*

*not of the world, even as I am not of it. Sanctify them
by the truth; your word is truth."*

John 17:15–17 (NIV)

Brian and I have had the experience of moving both boys
into dorm rooms as they took their next steps into man-
hood. Tanner is now across the country, and because he has
my grandchildren that is mighty far! My tears still come in
waves, contemplating the miles between this GiGi and that
precious family.

Jake was the most recent to head nine hours south to attend Texas A&M. I will say it was anything but pretty when
I shut my Tahoe door and Brian drove us away. But it would
have been impossible for this very weak and emotional mom
had I not known a few things about this young man.

He knows whose he is.

He knows who he is.

He believes that God is who He says he is.

He believes God can do all He says He can do.

Jake knows he can do all things through Christ who gives
him strength. (adapted from Beth Moore, *Believing God*)[1]

For years, Brian and I watched Jake become familiar with
his sword, the Word of God. We watched him try to use it,
unsure in the beginning, but the Word never returns void.
The power is in the Weapon itself. And then we watched as
the warrior, our Jake, began to recognize the power of the
Spirit within him.

And now, we have watched him face down giants in his
own life, wielding his sword like a skilled warrior, under-

standing the strength within him (the Spirit of God) and the strength he holds in his hands (the Word of God). He has done this while giving all the glory to the Lord.

We are raising Joshuas, those who understand the importance and the power of lingering in God's presence. In the presence of the Father, our sons gain His perspective and they begin to understand His heart. They learn to wield the sword and they receive their calling, their assignments.

Raising warriors...that's our assignment.

Joshua has a message for us moms, as well.

The Israelites were moving into the Promised Land, and the walls of Jericho still stood. But even before that faith-filled, valiant march around the city, there were obstacles. The first one they came to was the Jordan River, which we are told in Joshua 3:15 was at flood stage.

Have you ever felt like life was at flood stage? As the mom of two toddlers at home, just trying to keep everyone clean, fed and not playing in toilet water can feel like flood stage. The greatest accomplishment of the day could be taking a shower yourself! As a working mom, sending a baked item for the teacher's birthday, making sure your children have PE clothes and lunch money, dealing with an unexpected and untimely case of acne, and getting yourself ready for an 8:30 a.m. presentation, can't you feel the flood waters spraying your face? Or how about a mom raising teens? Trying to get them to move faster, drive slower, talk to you longer, talk to their friends less, enjoy school, enjoy that *certain* girl less, and pick up their room but with a good attitude — flood stages!

"And as soon as the priests who carry the ark of the Lord – the Lord of all the earth – set foot in the Jordan, its waters flowing downstream will be cut off and stand up in a heap."

Joshua 3:13 (NIV)

Recently, I made a trip to the mountains with my youngest two, Jake and Madi. My kids are just like yours; we face the same difficulties and temptations. We experience the same emotions. Just before heading off to Colorado, I began to say to the Lord, "I just need some space — room enough to move and breathe and connect with my kids. Life is so busy and overwhelming; if we can somehow push it back, create a little space of peace on dry ground, we can regain our footing and refill to move forward."

Joshua 3:13 ministered to this tired mama's heart. When the priests (that's us) who carry the ark of the Lord (His very Presence) into the flood waters of our lives, the waters flowing downstream will be cut off and stand in a heap. I focused on doing just that — inviting the presence and the peace of the Almighty to join us, to overshadow us, and to push back the flood. He did just that.

We laughed. We rested. We laughed. We hiked. We laughed. We ate. We laughed. We played — did I mention, we laughed? And I cried, because I was so thankful for the space in this busy life to experience two of those most dear to me, on dry ground.

We went on a day hike and saw some of the most beautiful creation of the Father. But I believe this was just for me.

"...Each of you is to take up a stone on his shoulder, according to the number of the tribes of the Israelites, to serve as a sign among you. In the future, when your children ask you, 'What do these stones mean?' tell them that the flow of the Jordan was cut off before the ark of the covenant of the Lord. When it crossed the Jordan, the waters of the Jordan were cut off. These stones are to be a memorial to the people of Israel forever."

Joshua 4:5–7 (NIV)

It was His Presence all the time.

"And Joshua the son of Nun was full of the spirit of wisdom, for Moses had laid his hands on him. So, the people of Israel obeyed him and did as the Lord had commanded Moses."

Deuteronomy 34:9

As we raise young men to honor those in authority over them, to honor their families and the values we hold dear, and most importantly to honor the Lord, we need to lay our hands on them. As a mother, your fingerprints are all over your family. You have held them during difficult times. You have held them by the arms as you spoke sternly to them when necessary. You have hugged them as you laughed and wiped mud and sweat from their faces. You are the mom of a warrior, of a Joshua.

Have you used those same tender hands to bless your son? Have you had him bow his head in honor of the Lord while you placed your tender hand on his head and spoke life over him? He needs you to bless him. To remind him of who he is called to be. To tell him that he is capable, he is strong enough. He knows how to use his weapons for the giants he will face and the battles he must fight. Release him to do exactly what the Lord is asking of him, to become a man of honor. Believe all of it for him until he can believe it for himself.

"The tongue has the power of life and death..." (Proverbs 18:21 NIV). Speak life to that boy of yours.

He will be encouraged, blessed and touched by many people in his life. But the fingerprints of a warrior mom will always be evident on his heart.

Joshua was a man of honor. He was a man who was regarded with great respect and fulfilled the call of God on his life. In this section, we discuss teaching our sons to honor their wives and families, to honor their own calling and identity, and to honor the Lord Himself.

15

Wife and Family

"My mother was the most beautiful woman I ever saw. All I am I owe to my mother. I attribute all of my success in life to the moral, intellectual and physical education I received from her."
PRESIDENT GEORGE WASHINGTON

I have loved every moment with my boys. Both of them are now physically bigger and stronger than I am. I have laughed as I've watched them wrestle each other. I have watched in amazement as they learned new things, learned to fix things, and enjoyed the wonder of a night sky. We have chased bugs, dogs, and each other. I have laughed with them until we cried, and cried with them over some monumental life changes. They are my boys, and I am so proud of them.

Have you ever considered the fact that you are the first woman that your son ever thought was beautiful? You are the first woman that your son expressed love for and received love from? A mother demonstrates for her sons what nurturing, gentleness, selflessness, grace, strength, peace, beauty, and love look like and how to live them out. What a powerful role you play in the life of that incredible young man!

You as his mother are a template for what his wife will someday resemble, right down to the way he should expect to be treated as a husband and how he should treat his wife. Your son is watching how you speak, how you deal with stress, how you carry yourself, and how you love your husband. One of the most important roles of a mother with sons is to model a godly woman.

Your relationship with Christ speaks volumes to your son. When he knows that you are up early before the house comes alive, spending time with the Savior, it will bring him great comfort and peace. He will recognize where your help comes from and will respect you for it. If your relationship with Christ isn't most important, why should his be? Your son watches, and he takes it all in. If he knows that you seek the throne room of the Almighty on his behalf and then you linger as the Father whispers plans and callings for that young man to his mother, it will matter to him.

A godly woman chases hard after Jesus. Though I am tempted to find comfort in Blue Bell chocolate ice cream when things get stressful and overwhelming, I most often don't. There is a young man watching. Someday when he is grown and with a family of his own, I want him to remember that when times were hard and overwhelming, his mom would put the spoon down and pick up her sword, the Word of God, instead. There will always be time for ice cream, but as a godly wife and mother, some days there are battles to fight.

> *"Charm is deceptive, and beauty is fleeting; but a woman who fears the Lord is to be praised."*
>
> Proverbs 31:30 (NIV)

Physical beauty is in abundance in our society. Now can I just say that I am 100% against the idea of no makeup, long dresses, and buns? That is not what I am talking about. But one thing that breaks my heart is to see mothers dressing in an immodest and inappropriate fashion. Dress in a way that represents your husband, your sons (and your daughters, for that matter) with grace and dignity. Your son will not only learn from your example as he seeks his own bride, but he will love you for it.

New age spots and wrinkles seem to be appearing on a daily basis for this mom. I am not old, and I am determined not to act like I am either. To be perfectly honest, though, it stinks to look in the mirror and realize that I am no longer the younger person in the room, on the committee, or serving at my church. I am in my forties, and my youngest children are in college. I have four grandchildren who really do see me as a grandparent even if I insist on a more hip name like GiGi. Can you believe that? Though I try harder than I did in my 20s to be healthy and as fit as I can be, my body is 40-something and not 20-something, and it doesn't look the same in a bathing suit or yoga pants as it did back then.

But I have decided there is something beautiful about aging. My husband has loved me and been faithful to me for more than 20 years. He has watched my appearance change from a young newlywed, to a pregnant mommy, to a young mom exhausted from sleepless nights with infants and toddlers, to a taxi driver with messy hair and no time to cook dinner so fast food again (scowl). He has loved me and seen me as beautiful when I got impetigo on my lip from my wrestler boys (true story) and when I got a black eye from playing catch with them in the front yard (also a true story).

Bottom line is, my husband thinks I am beautiful. My sons look at me and see their mom, and they love me too. I want my sons to remember me sweaty because I was helping them work in the yard or muddy from helping them push their car out of the ditch. I want the boys to remember me in the stands with tears streaming down my face in pride, and I want them to recall me dressed up and elegant at their high school graduation. I want them to remember me as beautiful in all of those moments because someday I want them to look across the lawn at another young newlywed with sweat and dirt on her face and see her as pure beauty as well.

Honor your son's dad. Society mocks fathers. So many TV shows and movies portray men and fathers as incompetent, lazy, silly, and ignorant. A young man looks up to his dad, and he should. His father is his example of what a man should be — how he should love and protect his bride, giving himself for her, and how he should nurture, teach, and raise his family. Dads model a good work ethic and healthy friendships and life choices for their sons. Dad is often his son's first hero. As mothers, we need to recognize and appreciate the strength our sons gain from their fathers.

I love to leave notes. I do it often. When my sons were having a difficult time, when we had a disagreement, or maybe even when something amazing happened, I would leave notes for them. And some could be elaborate. I would search for the right paper and pen color. Of course, it needed to be in my handwriting and not typed. For Pete's sake, we have journals full of our notes back and forth that I prayed the Lord would use to reach them when I was not with them. Words are valuable to me, and I have worked hard to communicate that to my sons. By their calculations I have used a ton of them!

One day, I saw a white Post-it note from my husband to one of the boys. It simply said, "You are enough. You have what it takes. I am proud of you. Love, Dad."

The note was taped to my son's desk. When I asked about it, I said something like, "Umm son, just curious, why is that note taped to your desk? I mean, I have written some pretty awesome notes on pretty paper, and they aren't taped to your desk."

My son said, "Mom, I love your notes. But when Dad says he's proud of me, it means something different."

Don't steal those moments from your son by belittling his father to him.

We can't interfere in their relationship. Allow your son's father to teach him to be a man; after all, that is his job. Notice I am saying "your son's father" here and not "your husband"? Whether you are married to your son's father or not, you can support and encourage their relationship. I am certainly not talking about supporting a neglectful and abusive father, but most dads aren't that. You may not have been able to remain married to his father, but regardless, he is your son's father and always will be. Don't make it difficult on your son. It is better for everyone if your son has a strong, healthy relationship with his dad. You can support their bond. Don't put your son in the middle. Your son feels protective of his mom and loyal to his dad. Make things easy on that boy of yours, and don't cause him to pick a side. Make the decision to be on his side — that's the best place to be.

Being truly committed to your marriage and modeling a healthy, strong marriage are the best things you can do for your son as he prepares for a marriage and family of his own someday. Don't fall into the trap of believing that when the waves rise and the skies darken, the truths in God's Word about marriage, covenant, and perseverance are suddenly for everyone else but you. Don't fall into the trap of believing that no other marriages have experienced hard times in the same way that you are, or that your situation must be different. So many times, I have heard couples say, "The Lord told me to divorce." or "I am sure He will make an exception this once because we are miserable." It is at that point that you need the anchor more than ever.

You see, no one needs an anchor when there are blue skies, a soft breeze, and smooth sailing. You need the anchor when you can't see the shore, the waves steal your breath, and you feel alone. It is in the dark moments when you need the anchor of His Word. Your sons, your family, and your friends are counting on you. When the storm approaches in their lives, they will reach for your hand.

It is no wonder that believers are referred to as children of God, heirs with Christ. Family is a source of strength, security, belonging, peace, and love. Make no mistake, all couples have difficult seasons. There is no such thing as a perfect marriage; we all struggle at points. But remember that your marriage is truly an anchor that holds your family and friends tightly in place when the storms of life hit.

"Shortly before dawn Jesus went out to them, walking on the lake. When the disciples saw him walking on the lake, they were terrified. 'It's a ghost,' they said and cried out in fear.

But Jesus immediately said to them: 'Take courage! It is I. Don't be afraid.'

'Lord, if it's you,' Peter replied, 'tell me to come to you on the water.'

'Come,' he said.'"

Matthew 14:25-29 (NIV)

There will be days that you would choose the Blue Bell chocolate and eat the entire half gallon rather than spend another afternoon wielding that Sword. Or times when you know that if you were willing, you could wear that short skirt and tight top and look at least as good as Tommy's mom does. Certainly, there will be days when you want to point out that you disagree with your son's father and if it were up to you, you would have handled the situation completely differently. But remember, these are the very waves our Savior was drawn to.

Something beautiful occurs to me this very moment: He has set my feet, He has set your feet, on the edge of the largest, ugliest, filthiest, most perverse sea in the history of mankind. Perversion, immorality, insecurity, confusion, and fear abound, and not only splash up around our ankles but can soak us straight through. And He walks. Step by step, right out into the middle of it, because our sons happen to be fighting those same waves. He doesn't say, "Hey, mom, run home into the safety of your isolation."

Instead He says," Take courage…Come."

Our sons admire and respect us as their mothers, and they will use our example as they honor their wives and families someday. So, my sister, let's wipe the chocolate ice cream off our faces and take Him up on it. See you in the waves.

Identity and Calling

"Just because you're lost doesn't mean you say your compass is broken."
THE EDGE

D oes my son know *who* he is? I don't think there is a mom out there who hasn't asked that question. We feel such responsibility. We are responsible for meeting our sons' physical needs, for pointing them to Christ, for encouraging their passions, for fostering a healthy relationship with them, for loving them — and certainly there are many more we could add. But one thing that occurs to me is that we are *not* responsible for their calling, their purpose.

The purposes and callings of our children are not our responsibility. I don't know about you, but that sure relieved some pressure for me. *"For I know the plans I have for you declares the Lord..."* Jeremiah 29:11 (NIV). It's not for us to research or demand. It's between the two of them, your son and the Lord. Our God has a unique plan for our sons, and He's working His plan. Our part is to teach them to listen for the voice of the Lord. In my mind, God's favorite game is hide and seek. He loves thrill and loves to be found. Teach your son to love the search.

155

Callings or purposes are not "drummed up." Your calling, your spouse's calling, and your son's calling are not something that you have to orchestrate. Sure, you need to have a good work ethic. You need to set goals. You need to operate in excellence in all things as a good testimony of the King. But, moms, you can't create your own calling, much less that of your son. God simply leads each of you into it. Whatever His calling is for your son, God is already there. The precious feet of the Dream Giver firmly planted in the soil of that boy's inheritance, leading him there. The key is to see the Father and follow. Simple.

Callings aren't to be compared. As a mom, it sure is easy to see other young people and either compare your son to them or try and discount or diminish the other young man's accomplishments to make your son (or yourself) feel better. The fact is, the callings of others are to be celebrated because their greatness does not diminish the greatness of your son.

The apostle Peter asked the Lord about John's calling, saying, "What about him?"

> "Jesus answered, 'If I want him to remain alive until I return, what is that to you? You must follow me.'"
>
> John 21:22 (NIV).

God hasn't forgotten that precious son of yours. The Father has called him to something great, regardless of the callings of his peers.

For any mom who may be in a difficult season with a son and may be watching him struggle with his identity and purpose, do not be discouraged. Also, don't allow your son's struggle to increase the volume in your home or in your heart. Don't panic. Remain constant and steady. You walk in faith and in peace. He is listening and will gain much security from you.

However, you are not alone in this season. On a daily basis, I see young men who were raised in intact homes being swallowed up by peer pressure, poor decisions, our society, and sin, and their families being literally thrown into a tailspin. Often these families wake up and find themselves in a reality that is beyond their wildest imaginations.

I know the feeling of, "Where exactly are You taking him? Because this looks like a foreign land, in fact, much like a desert!" That feeling of worry as you watch your child walk through a difficult situation or process can be frightening and painful.

> *"Therefore, behold I will allure her; I bring her into the wilderness and speak tenderly to her.*
>
> *And there I will give her her vineyards. And make the Valley of Achor a door of hope. There she shall answer as in the days of her youth..."*
>
> Hosea 2:14-15

No one likes the wilderness, the desert. It's hot. The scenery is lacking. The food is bland, and there is a lot of grumbling; just ask Moses. It is difficult when you notice your own scenery start to change and realize that you are walking into a desert. But it is most difficult to watch as your son heads that direction! I love the word choice here: "I am now going to *allure* her; I will *lead* her into the desert." When I think of being "allured" or "led," I am thinking beach all the way!

But as I really consider it, though in my mind there are lots of negatives about the desert, there is something beautiful about it, as well. There are few distractions. Over and over in God's Word we see that He is moving us into a place of aloneness with Him. He desires to remove our distractions so that our focus can be fully on Him. It would appear to me that by the way the verse is worded, we may dread the desert experience, but it is beautiful to Him.

When you see, your son entering a desert season, encourage yourself with this Scripture in Hosea. God is never harsh or condemning. Even in difficult moments, God is always loving and merciful. He will speak tenderly to that son of yours. It's just that sometimes He refuses to allow our children (or us) to avoid dealing with a circumstance or situation and so He leads us gently to the desert where He can speak tenderly to us. He leads us to the place where He can love us.

The Valley of Achor means the "Valley of Trouble." So, this verse is literally saying, "I will make the valley of trouble a door of hope." That is beautiful to me, to realize that our very valley of trouble can be transformed into a door of hope and, oh, the singing and celebration that will commence!

> *"We should go up and take possession of the land, for we can certainly do it."*
>
> Numbers 13:30 (NIV)

I know what my God is capable of. He is capable of redemption, restoration, forgiveness, rebuilding, orchestrating, blessing, and pouring out unbelievable love and mercy. Do not give up the land that is your spiritual inheritance, the land that you, as a mom, have fought so hard to gain.

I may not know the situation unique to you and your family. Your desires, prayers, concern, and pain are very personal. What I do know is that the Lord is faithful and He is at work in the life of your son. Though things change, people change, our children change, situations change, dreams change, images change, prayers change, and lives change — there is one thing that is constant. One grip of which we can be sure, one thing that is common to us all: the Lord never changes. He is the same yesterday, today, and forever. The Lord has done great things among us, and there is more to do. The Lord can save, forgive, and change our sons. He can change us.

God sees potential. He sees the plans that He has for our sons, and these young men are destined for greatness.

"Just because you're lost doesn't mean you say your compass is broken." *The Edge*

My, has this statement been rolling over and over in my heart and mind. This is the perfect picture of our culture in general. We are lost, and not only have we declared our compass broken, but we have surmised that anyone who thinks there is a true north, who believes that compasses do give us direction, and who tries to point people down the safest path is hate-filled and closed-minded.

We must not grow weary in speaking identity and purpose over and to our sons. As mothers, our hearts are full of hope and love for our families. Mamas want nothing more than to protect our children from all of the ugliness and corruption of our world. We are willing to read, pray, study, listen to those older and wiser, and do anything for the good of our families. My encouragement to you is, don't stop.

> *"And let us not grow weary of doing good, for in due season we will reap if we do not give up."*
>
> Galatians 6:9

There will be days when our sons feel lost, when they don't know which way is north. The compass is not broken. We must be diligent in returning to the Word and seeking the Lord's counsel as we guard what has been entrusted to us. Some days, we moms are simply exhausted. Remember to remain as diligent when those boys are thirteen as you were when they were three. Remind yourself that the reason you set standards at age seven was because you knew fifteen was coming. There are so many other moms who are with you to support you and help hold up your arms.

Do not let your shield of faith rest on the ground and do not set your Sword aside. The battle rages. If you fight, you will certainly win. But fight you must. When you are lost, the Compass (God's Word) shows true north. This is a marathon and not a sprint, but precious moms, RUN. Run the race to win the prize and do not stop short of that finish line! Listen closely, and you will hear the cheers of encouragement from the moms who have gone this way before you.

One morning a few years ago, as I was backing out of the driveway to take Jake and Madison to school, I looked over on the side of our house where we have two bushes. The bushes were several years old and had certainly had time to grow and look like bushes. I'll just say up front, having a green thumb is not one of my talents. But as we looked over at the bushes, I wanted to chuckle because it was springtime when buds and blooms should begin to appear. The little bushes were trying to grow and flourish, but they basically looked like sticks stuck in the ground. As we passed by, it just struck me as funny and I said to the kids, "I think somebody forgot to tell them that they are bushes!" As we drove to school, the Lord began to speak to me about that.

Moms, we declare identity over our sons; we tell them who they are. We want our sons to grow into young men with certain values, morals, and beliefs. What happens to our sons if we don't tell them who they are? What happens if we stop declaring identity to them?

It's important that we take time to tell our sons who they are. We need to take the time to declare over them that the Word of God says He gives His angels charge over them. He goes before and behind them. God covers them with His wings. The Bible describes our sons as being more than conquerors and equipped for every good work prepared in advance for them to do.

God is the creator of all things, the breath of life. He is the beginning and He is the end. He has written every chapter of the book of your boy's life, and He placed in him a desire for adventure, a desire for a journey, a desire to win, and a desire to make something of himself.

As a society, we do a pretty good job of teaching children how to be strong physically. It is a priority in our culture, as it should be, to teach our young people how to make their physical bodies strong. Yet we have a very difficult time teaching kids how to be strong on the inside.

If a young person wants to be a wrestler, we teach him endurance. We teach him strength and wrestling moves that can be effective. We tell him that his core needs to be strong, so crunches are in order. We teach him deliberately all of the things it takes to be a good athlete or musician.

But do we tell our sons what it means to be a leader? Do we know how to train them to be leaders? Do we train them to share Christ with their friends? Do we train them to teach or to show compassion? Do we train them to practice self-control or perseverance? Oh, that our sons would have perseverance! Everything does not come to us fast and easy. Oftentimes the things that we work the hardest for bring the greatest reward and fulfillment.

Can you imagine the difference in our culture if we raised our young men to be strong on the inside and outside? What if we raised a generation that loved adventure, practiced self-control, compassion, and perseverance — a generation that took God at His Word and took up the full armor of God? These young people would run their race with strength and honor. My heart is so full of emotion as I imagine it!

I want my own sons to run so hard that they lose their breath. I want them to strive for things, to sometimes attain and sometimes fall short because there is great benefit to both. I want my guys to dance in the rain and enjoy a sunset. I want them to love deeply and keep their word. I want them to influence their friends and point them to Christ. I want my sons to go to bed and sleep soundly because they lived the day fully. I want them to run their race and use everything that God has placed in them for His glory. I want them to leave it all here, to crawl across the finish line with dirt under their nails because they dared to truly live.

I pray the very same for your sons, as well. Declare it.

Honoring the Lord

> *"Then the Lord said to Moses, 'Write this as a memorial in a book and recite it in the ears of Joshua, that I will utterly blot out the memory of Amalek from under heaven.'"*
> *EXODUS 17:14*

I love the phrase, *"recite it in the ears of Joshua."* In the NIV it says, *"make sure Joshua hears it."* If we back up in the passage just slightly, we will find the story of the battle between the Israelites and Amalek. Moses told Joshua, *"Choose for us men and go out and fight Amalek. Tomorrow I will stand on the top of the hill with the staff of God in my hand"* (Exodus 17:9). During the battle, as long as Moses's hand was raised, the Israelites prevailed; when his arms dropped, Amalek prevailed. Aaron and Hur helped to hold Moses's arms high, and the Israelites were victorious. Then the Lord said, "Write it down, and be sure that Joshua hears it."

It would do us a world of good to take just a moment, put the book down, and remember the times in our lives when we have stood in each of these different places in a spiritual battle. I know you have, and so have I. I can recall moments when I was in the trenches, blood and tears in abundance, desperately trying to see through the maddening chaos and

163

catch a glimpse of my mentor on the mountain, hands lifted high. Being able to lock eyes with someone who was standing strong in trust and faith for me, even in the midst of the fighting — at times that was exactly what I needed to continue. My thoughts are flooded with times when I have been the one worshiping, honoring, and standing while my children or those I am blessed to mentor swing their swords. Those times when I am privileged to petition the throne room and intercede for those precious to me are some of the moments that are nearest to my heart.

"...Make sure that Joshua hears it" or *"recite it in the ears of Joshua"* — now, that is holy ground. I wonder if we understand the magnitude of the spiritual necessity to remind our sons of the times when we honored the Lord, when we put Him first, when we held our arms up in honor and praise even if it meant having others literally lift them for us? Or maybe even more importantly, do we pass on to our boys *how* we practically honor the Lord in our lives?

Certainly, demonstrating to our sons the ways that we honor the Lord with our lives will be different at each phase of their development. When the boys were young, we had a routine with most things. I've always believed there is such value in structure. It was important to me that we talked about the Lord, read Bible stories, and memorized stories and Scripture when they were old enough. But equally important was demonstrating a personal and intimate relationship with the Lord. Each evening we would pray together. I would pray, and then each of my children would say their own prayers out loud. Often, we would use anointing oil, and they would pray for me or for each other. It was very special to them, and they loved it. In a practical and demonstrative way, we were honoring the Lord with our lives.

As they grew to be middle school and high school students, we would often ask the question, "What would honor the Lord in this situation?" If they were struggling with a coach or having a difficult season with a friend, we would ask, "What would honor the Lord here?" Sometimes it is easy to spiritualize a situation by saying things like "we walk by faith and not by sight" or "in our home we honor the Lord." But what does that mean in a practical sense? It means that we treat others the way the Lord would want us to, even when we would just as soon punch their lights out. It means saying, "Son, rather than going to the school and giving that coach a piece of my mind, we are going to honor his position and ask the Lord to bless him." Taking the time to talk through feelings with our sons is important and necessary, but being able to "hold up our arms" as they face battles is most important. We must be able to transition from focusing on how hurt or angry they are in a way that honors the Lord.

As our boys become young men, we need to open our hearts and allow ourselves to be vulnerable as we share with our sons the ways that we intentionally keep Christ on the throne of our hearts. They will need to develop their own relationship with Christ, but we can give them an idea of what it looks like. Not too long ago, a young man that the Lord has placed in my family's life asked me if I would share with him what my personal time with the Lord looks like. I would like to briefly share with you what I shared with him.

"But as it is written, 'What no eye has seen, nor ear heard, nor the heart of a man imagined, what

God has prepared for those who love Him' – these things God has revealed to us through the Spirit. For the Spirit searches everything, even the depths of God."

1 Corinthians 2:9-10

Truly the simplest desire of my heart is that the Lord would consider me enough that He would share secrets with me and take me to the depths of who He is.

My times with the Lord...

Most often, I begin with worship, and I have to move around. I get distracted easily, so I walk all over the house or backyard. And I worship and "talk" to Him. I'm not sure if it's "prayer" even. I say things like, "I blew it and I'm not yet sorry!" Or "I think there's a better idea then You moving my kids nine hours away..." or "I'm so mad I could spit or cuss" or "I'm scared to death." I believe that God is big enough to handle my truthful communication with Him.

"For I received from the Lord what I also passed on to you: The Lord Jesus, on the night he was betrayed, took bread, and when he had given thanks, he broke it and said, 'This is my body, which is for you; do this in remembrance of me.' In the same way, after supper he took the cup, saying, 'This cup is the new covenant in my blood; do this, whenever you drink it, in remembrance of me.' For whenever you eat this bread and drink this cup, you proclaim the Lord's death until he comes."

1 Corinthians 11:23-26 (NIV)

Secondly, I almost always take communion. The bread reminds me of the bride price He paid for me. He paid for my transgressions (when I break the rules.) He paid for my iniquity (my grossly immoral sins). And He purchased my health (physical, emotional, mental and spiritual). I ask Him to appropriate everything He purchased for me. I don't want to leave anything on the table unclaimed; I want to put it all into practice in my life.

Then the cup — the cup speaks of our value. In Jewish tradition, when a young man proposes to his bride, he offers a cup of wine. By receiving His cup, we are accepting His proposal. The cup says that He values me. He sees me as pure and beautiful and valuable. To receive the cup is to accept the blessing and responsibility of being His. And I ask Him to help me live my life in a way that demonstrates that.

You see, when Jesus reminded us to "remember" when we observe communion, He did not intend for us to only remember *that* He died, but to remember *why* He died. Our great Savior gave Himself as a sacrifice, "and did not open His mouth," to make an exchange. He exchanged our physical and mental weakness for His strength. He carried our sadness so that we could empty our hands of it to pick up peace and joy. He was pierced for every time we have broken a rule, and He was crushed for our grossly unfair behavior. His wounds purchased our healing. *Remember.*

I remind myself that: He exchanged my weakness for His strength. He carried the things that break my heart, and He hands me peace. He was pierced for all the times I have broken a rule, and He declares me innocent. He was crushed for my grossly unfair behavior, and He calls me to have a quiet and gentle spirit. His wounds bought my healing and the healing of my family.

Out loud, I will put on the armor of God described in Ephesians 6. Usually still walking around, still praying out loud, I put on the full armor piece by piece, speaking out what each accomplishes. "Thank You, Father, for the belt of truth around my waist, which is the center of my being, my core, and it brings balance. Lord, I thank You that peace covers my feet, and I don't move unless I move in Your peace," etc.

Romans 10:17 says, *"Faith comes from hearing and hearing through the word of Christ."* I need to speak life, promises, and hope over my own soul and so do you. Speaking truth and life has such power. Often, I will make an out-loud declaration that I am not afraid, even if I am. The Word tells us that we have not been given a spirit of fear, but of power, love, and a sound mind. I will not be motivated or held back by fear.

Then, I pray. I pray for anyone who comes to mind or that He places on my heart. I look up Scripture that comes to mind. Usually I will write the Scripture in my journal. At this point, the Lord will often bring people to mind, and if He does I try to text or call to let them know that I am praying.

During my prayer time, I will listen for promptings from the Holy Spirit. If I feel like there is an action that I need to take, I try and take the step. I have learned that I tend to overthink things, so I have disciplined myself that if He speaks, I move. If I wait, I have the tendency to talk myself out of it.

Your time with the Lord will look different from mine, and your son's certainly will. "Throw some mud on the wall for him," as my sweet friend would say. Give your son an idea of what it looks like to be deliberate in your pursuit of a relationship with Christ, to honor Him with your life.

My family and I love the mountains. When I was a child, my grandparents had a cabin in New Mexico, and my favorite thing was to pull into the mountains late on a Friday night. Smelling the mountain air, seeing the stars, and knowing that a relaxing weekend with my grandparents was on the horizon gave me an overwhelming sense of peace. My family and I still visit those same mountain towns a few times each year. I have been pondering the mountains and what it is that I love so much about them.

- Time moves more slowly in the mountains. You don't tend to see people scurrying around at quite the same pace as you do in the city.
- You can find alone places.
- In the mountains, you see beauty and gain perspective.
- There is the opportunity to rest, to simply abide. Busyness comes naturally to me. I have to train myself to just "be."
- You can see more from the vantage point of the high places, and you tend to notice more detail.

I love that the Father beckons us to come up higher. But as I think about it practically, it can be very daunting to approach the base of a mountain, knowing that the journey to the summit may be extremely difficult.

- No one can "carry" us to the mountain peak. We must make the journey ourselves.

- It is difficult and at some points may seem to be more than we can handle.
- The journey puts priorities in order. We don't carry unnecessary items up the mountain. It makes the burden too heavy.
- We summit the mountain on purpose. No one climbs a mountain by accident.
- It changes our perspective. We can see people and situations more clearly.

As we seek to know and honor the Father on a deeper level, to try and get a glimpse of His perspective, we begin our own personal journey to the High Places. I believe this a process that believers go through many times in their lifetimes. There is so much to be gained on the journey, no matter how difficult it may be.

I remember a trek up the mountain with my family a few years ago. As we sat down for lunch, our conversation changed my perspective forever. My children began to talk about all the beauty they had seen on the way up. As I listened to them, I realized that all I could remember seeing were the rocks we had to climb over and the dirt under my feet. I was focused on the trail, focused on the difficulty. What the Lord spoke to me that day was that even in the journey, my focus must be on the destination. Even in our struggles, if we will only lift up our heads, there is beauty around us to help sustain us.

I don't know where you or your son are in your journey, but I am praying that you are on the trail to the High Places. The High Places are where we are so near to Him that we can hear Him whisper plans and perspective to us. The High Places are where He fills us up and equips us for the next calling. Don't give up. Don't stop. Pursue Him.

A beautiful worship song by Hillsong called "Highlands (Song of Ascent)" says, "You're the summit where my feet are."[1] Wherever He is, in the valley or the peaks — He is the destination.

I will see you on the trail…to the High Places.

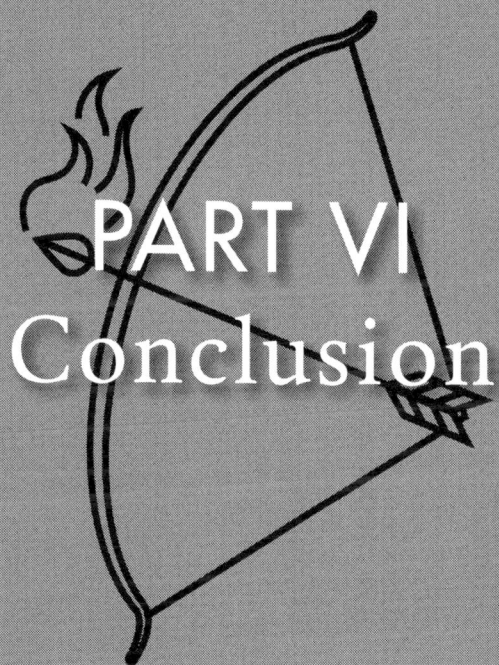

PART VI
Conclusion

Tension to Target

"You are braver than you believe, stronger than you seem, and smarter than you think."
CHRISTOPHER ROBIN TO WINNIE THE POOH

T he process of working on a new project or book is always overwhelming to me. I am not good at it, and it causes me angst. This project has been different in only one way. Though I do not enjoy the process and my skill set has remained consistently lacking, I am passionate about my relationship with my sons and that has been the driving force behind the emotion and time that has been poured into this book. The boys have been with us the entire way — encouraging me, laughing with me, listening to me cry, and praying, not only for me but for you too. I asked both of my sons to write a letter to you.

Here you go.

From Tanner...

Mom,

Remember when I was short on rent money, and I asked you and Dad to help pay the bill?

175

You told me no.

I was stressed because it was due in just a couple of days! You knew I was struggling. You knew the odds were stacked against me. You knew there was a possibility that Bracen, Whitney and I would get evicted. But you still said no.

I want you to know that there hasn't been a single moment in my life more beneficial than hearing Dad tell me, "I'm sorry, son, but Mom and I have decided not to help you with the money. I hope you understand."

Yes, I did understand! And just like you knew I would, I pushed my "poor me" attitude aside and made it happen. I know it was an EXTREMELY tough decision for you to make because it wasn't about the rent money or just "teaching me a lesson." It was about helping me become a wiser and stronger man. If I haven't told you before, I'm telling you now; you made the right decision!

The lesson I learned from you and Dad that day changed my life. It changed the way I think, the way I work, the way I act, and most importantly the way I mentor my own children!

Thanks, Mom. Love you to the moon!

To the moms reading this book, now that I have children of my own, I understand that parenting is no joke! It's hard! No, changing a diaper is not hard, getting them ready for school is not hard, and helping them decide what college to go to isn't hard either (well maybe 😁).

What is hard is dealing with the fear of failure. There's a constant thought of, "I should have han-

dled it like this," "I shouldn't have said that," "I wish I would have..."

These kinds of thoughts will always run through our minds no matter what, even if others view us as perfect parents.

With that said, please don't be afraid to make decisions that might make you look like the bad guy. If you know it's in your child's best interest, do it. They might fight and complain because they aren't getting their way, but deep down they know you have the right intentions.

When my mom and dad told me they weren't helping me with my rent payment, I was upset. I wasn't upset with them personally, though. I knew that it tore them up inside to say no, but that's what makes them strong parents. The easy decision would have been to bail me out and just pay the rent, but fortunately my parents weren't afraid of making the hard decision. I am a stronger man for it.

Keep fighting the good fight,
Tanner Gibbs

From Jake....

Hey Mom,

It is difficult for me to describe our relationship, but it is priceless to me. I truly believe that our relationship has been instrumental in shaping me into the man I am today.

Growing up with you as my mom was always an adventure. You always made sure to fill our home with laughter and love. As I was growing up, I got to watch you and Dad pursue the Lord and teach Tanner, Madi and me what it looks like to have a personal relationship with Jesus. That is something I could never be thankful enough for.

From a young age, you always pushed me to be better, to work harder, and to care for others. I always knew that I had a shoulder to cry on when I fell off my bike and scraped my knee, when Tanner went a little too hard roughhousing, after a tough loss in a wrestling match, or when I just felt brokenhearted. But I knew I couldn't cry for too long before you would pick me up, dust me off, and tell me to keep going. You taught me that life is not easy, but there is strength in the Lord.

You always believed in me and helped teach me to reject passivity. "You are the tip of the sword" you would tell me, and send me off to fight the next battle. You were always there to comfort me, but you never babied me, and you taught me what a real man looks like. You taught me to trust the Lord at all times and to lean on Him in times of trouble and prosperity. Thank you for teaching me how to listen to the Lord's voice. I always really enjoy getting to have spiritual conversations with you and to talk deeply about the Lord's Word.

Even though we worked hard, we always had time for some fun. I will always cherish the movie nights, card games, and all the dumb ideas, but what

I remember and liked most were our one-on-one talks. Thank you for always taking the time to talk and being willing to talk at any time. You always put Tanner, Madi and me ahead of yourself.

Although I could go on and on, I want to keep it short. Thank you, Mom, for your love, compassion, encouragement, and your sacrifice. I will always love you and be there for you (even if you do end up in the Villages 😊).

I want to encourage all the moms who may be reading this. I know that it is hard to be a mom, and it can be hard to find hope when it feels like a storm is going on around you. You may feel like you are messing everything up. Believe me, it wasn't always a smooth ride between me and my mom, but keep believing in your son because he needs you! Keep trusting in the Lord and praying for your son. The dreams that the Lord has for him are far greater than you could ever imagine. It may not seem like your son is listening, but I promise he is. No matter how mad or frustrated he may get, he loves you and you will always have that special place in his heart. Trust me. Keep fighting and finish the race the Lord has laid out before you.

I am praying for you,
Jake Gibbs

When I read the letters that my boys wrote, it is hard to describe the emotions that surface. I am so proud of them and thankful for all of the struggles and the victories over the years. They are men now, and their words and encouragement are like a deep breath after a long run and a healing balm to my soul. I am praying that you hold on to hope. I pray that you will hear words like these from your sons one day. The days are long, and the years are short, and all of the sacrifice, tears and joy that are left in the wake of raising these mighty men do not go unnoticed. I wrote a letter to my boys when they were two and nine years old. It still hangs in Jake's room today. I would like to share it with you.

Heroes

I have been considering all of the immorality and lack of values in our culture, and I have been praying for you. I wonder who your heroes will be. Who will you look up to?

Our great President George Washington said, "The time is at hand which must determine whether Americans are to be free men or slaves." As much as I hate it, the time is now. Will you choose to be free or will you choose to be bound by peer pressure and temptation?

President Abraham Lincoln said, "My dream is of a place in time where America will once again be seen as the last, best hope on earth." That can happen and it starts with you making choices of honor and character.

There have been many great men in our past. Who will be the great men of the future?

The history of your life has yet to be written, and each day you pen a chapter of your life with your actions. You display your beliefs and priorities through everything that you are a part of. You can be any-

thing that you are willing to work to become, and there are two things that Dad and I want for you.

Know and love the Lord Jesus with all your heart, soul and strength.

Find His purpose for your life and fulfill it.

To do that, you must surrender everything to Him. President Theodore Roosevelt said, "No man is worth his salt who is not willing at all times to risk his life in a great cause." Be worth your salt.

Work hard to accomplish His purpose for your life. "For I know the plans I have for you, declares the Lord, plans to prosper you and not to harm you, plans to give you hope and a future." Jeremiah 29:11 (NIV). Do not allow the enemy to steal that truth from you. Work hard at knowing the heart of God. Vince Lombardi said, "The harder you work, the harder it is to surrender."

So, as I contemplate heroes and ask God to give you someone to look up to, the answer is all too clear. As I pictured our Savior on the cross, the following verse came to mind.

"All authority on heaven and earth has been given to me; therefore, go and make disciples of all nations, baptizing them in the name of the Father, Son and Holy Spirit and teaching them to obey everything I have commanded you. And surely I am with you always to the very end of the age"

(Matthew 28:18-20 NIV).

We love you and are committed to interceding for you always. We are proud and honored to be your par-

ents. You are never alone. We leave you in the hands of the hero, your heavenly Father and trust that He will have His way with you. Be a great man of the future.

Love,
Mom and Dad

I would say the Lord is faithful because these two man cubs that the Lord entrusted to this mama have sure become friends and heroes to me.

"Unless the Lord builds the house, those who build it labor in vain. Unless the Lord watches over the city, the watchman stays awake in vain. It is vain that rise up early and go late to rest, eating the bread of anxious toil; for he gives to his beloved sleep. Behold, children are a heritage of the Lord, the fruit of the womb a reward. Like arrows in the hand of a warrior are the children of one's youth. Blessed is the man who fills his quiver with them! He shall not be put to shame when he speaks with his enemies in the gate"

Psalm 127

I first fell in love with and clung to this Psalm when Jake was a colicky baby and sleep was escaping us all. *"He gives to his beloved sleep,"* I would declare in Jesus' name! And then again I clung to these words when there were elementary and middle school worries and homework that kept us awake into the wee hours of the night. Then came the teen years: *"Unless the Lord builds the house, we labor in vain,"* and *"eating the bread of anxious toil is vain"*…yet, sleep still evaded us.

It's the tension.

These young men are truly arrows in our quivers, and all their lives we sharpen them by teaching them to communicate, to build strong relationships, and to love the Lord with all of their being. Then comes the season when we remove that arrow and steady it into the bow as we prepare to release it. The tension is necessary and must not be mistaken as a negative. You see, when we prepare to release an arrow, tension between the bow and arrow is necessary; it's part of the process.

Be encouraged as you prepare for your own *release* of sorts. There will be tension. Our sons need to find their passion, while we steady their thoughts. Our sons will begin to decide what type of friends they will choose, while we give insight and input. Our sons must begin to make decisions about the university they will attend or even *if* they will attend, while we offer support and encouragement. Our sons will begin to wear out the carpet next to their beds, while we continue to settle quickly into the worn places from years of use next to ours. And we will continue to draw the bow and absorb the tension. Because that's our job, to absorb the tension, to set our aim, to steady our hand, and set our faces like flint. This is what you were born to do — you are a mother.

As a mother, you are strong and gentle, bold and humble, full of excitement for your son's future and heartbroken for the change that same future means for yours. You are full of love, respect and hope for your son, and though the tension is difficult and the release will be initially overwhelming, you will release that arrow. And he will soar into his destiny, his calling — because that's what an arrow does. Due to your strength, support, and aim, your arrow will fly true. Because that's what your son was born to do.

Ephesians tells us that our God has prepared good works in advance for us to do, for our sons to do. As our sons deepen their trust in and relationship with the Father, the Lord will ignite a flame deep within them. And our arrows, on fire with love and passion for the Lord, when released, will start a fire that cannot be contained. They will hit the target.

Good job, mama. Now, steady, draw that bow. Release.

Notes

Chapter 7 - Relationship

1. John Eldredge, *Wild at Heart* (Thomas Nelson Publishers, 2001)

Chapter 8 - Prayer

1. Philip Harrelson, "Take Him to His Mother" (sermon), September 27, 2004, https://www.sermoncentral.com/sermons/take-him-to-his-mother-philip-harrelson-sermon-on-mothers-day-72324

Chapter 9 – Adventure

1. Jim Grassi, *Building a Ministry of Spiritual Mentoring* (Thomas Nelson Publishers, 2014), 111
2. Grassi, 111
3. Grassi, 111
4. Philip Zimbardo, Nikita D. Coulombe, *The Demise of Guys: Why Boys Are Struggling and What We Can Do About It* (e-book, Amazon Digital Services LLC, May 23, 2012)
5. Zimbardo, Coulombe
6. Zimbardo, Coulombe

Chapter 11 - Communication

1. The Washington Post, "Teens spend nearly nine hours every day consuming media," November 2015, https://www.

washingtonpost.com/news/the-switch/wp/2015/11/03/teens-spend-nearly-nine-hours-every-day-consuming-media/?utm_term=.3309ab6fffde

2. Common Sense Media, "New Report Finds Teens Feel Addicted to Their Phones, Causing Tension at Home," May 2016, https://www.commonsensemedia.org/about-us/news/press-releases/new-report-finds-teens-feel-addicted-to-their-phones-causing-tension-at

Chapter 12 - Purity

1. Sara Israelsen-Hartley, "Figuring out why teens turn to pornography," Deseret News, February 2, 2016, https://www.deseretnews.com/article/865646668/Addiction-label-may-delay-teens-recovery-from-online-porn.html

2. Fight the New Drug, "How Many People Are On Porn Sites Right Now? (Hint: It's a Lot)," May 24, 2019, https://fightthenewdrug.org/by-the-numbers-see-how-many-people-are-watching-porn-today/

3. Fight the New Drug

4. Fight the New Drug

5. Fight the New Drug

6. Fight the New Drug, "One in 10 Visitors to Hard-Core Porn Sites Is Under 10 Years Old, Study Shows," July 30, 2018, https://fightthenewdrug.org/data-says-one-in-10-visitors-to-porn-sites-are-under-10-years-old/

7. Fight the New Drug, "Here's the Shocking Percentage of 12-Year-Olds Who Admit They Struggle with Porn," September 13, 2017, https://fightthenewdrug.org/the-percentage-of-12-year-olds-who-admit-being-addicted-to-porn-will-shock-you/

8. Resource Center for Adolescent Pregnancy Prevention, "2015 Teen Sexual Activity Statistics," http://recapp.etr.org/recapp/index.cfm?fuseaction=pages.StatisticsDetail&PageID=555#-footer3

9. Candy Gibbs, *Rescue: Raising Teens in a Drowning Culture* (Fedd Books, 2014)

10. Jimmy Evans, *Marriage on the Rock: God's Design for Your Dream Marriage* (MarriageToday, 2018)

Chapter 13 – Fight

1. Barna, August 2016, https://onenewsnow.com/missions/2016/08/28/barna-only-3-percent-of-teens-read-bible-daily

Chapter 14 – Joshua

1. Beth Moore, *Believing God* (Lifeway Christian Resources, 2003)

Chapter 17 – Honoring the Lord

1. Hillsong, *Highlands: Song of Ascent,* words and music by Joel Houston & Benjamin Hastings, ©2018 Hillsong Music Publishing CCLI: 7122399

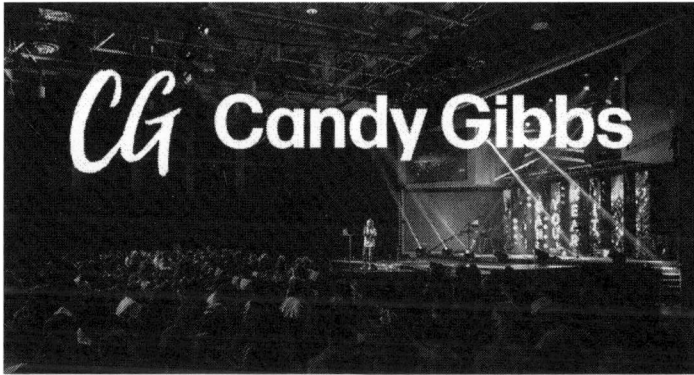

Candy is a powerful and dynamic speaker who
brings bold truth amidst a "tip-toeing" culture.

For more resources and to book
Candy for your next event, visit:
www.candygibbs.com